Praise for John Annoni and Beyond One Day

"If there is a more meaningful mission in the outdoors I've not heard about it." - **Ronnie "Cuz" Strickland, Senior Vice President of Mossy Oak TV & Video Production**

"His graduates told me one by one they'd be dead or in jail if it wasn't for John." This made John one of my heroes, too." - **Frank Miniter, New York Times bestselling author of The Ultimate Man's Survival Guide**

"I am always amazed by how much passion John has for youth and Camp Compass, especially after the length of time he has been doing it." - **Harold Luther, Cabela's Retail Marketing Manager**

"This book, like his work, will tell a story that creates opportunities for others and makes the world a better place for our kids." - **Pat Mundy, Leupold & Stevens Inc. Director of Brand Communications**

"An extraordinary framework for achievement that's easy to understand and could be applied to anything from starting a new business to running a country." - **Jim Shepherd, Editor/Publisher The Outdoor Wire Digital Network**

BEYOND ONE DAY

CAMP COMPASS ACADEMY'S
FRAMEWORK FOR FOSTERING THE
SOCIAL AND ACADEMIC
DEVELOPMENT OF AMERICA'S YOUTH

JOHN F. ANNONI

Beyond One Day—CCA's Framework for Fostering
the Social and Academic Development of America's Youth

Copyright © 2015 by John Annoni & CCA Inc.

All rights reserved. No part of this book may be reproduced
or transmitted in any form or by any means without written
permission from the author.

ISBN 978-0-692-30245-3

This book was printed in the USA by CCA Inc.

Dedication

To all of you aspiring to make the world a better place—especially for our youth.

Table of Contents

ACKNOWLEDGEMENTS..9

PREFACE...11

CHAPTER ONE: Introduction 15
A. Today's Youth, Parents or Guardians, and Society 15
B. America: Preserving Its Outdoor Sports Traditions/Heritage
     and Conserving Its Environment 19

CHAPTER TWO: Getting Involved With Youth and
     Programs for Them 21
A. Finding and Keeping Good People 21

CHAPTER THREE: Camp Compass Academy (CCA) 29
A. The Start 29
B. Who We Are and What We Do 36
C. Personnel/Shareholders and Their Roles and Responsibilities 37

CHAPTER FOUR: CCA Program Goals, Stages, and
     Special Emphases 61
A. Specific Program Goals 61
B. Program's Five Stages 62
C. Special Program Emphases 66

CHAPTER FIVE: Curriculum Approach, Development and
     Execution 75
A. Curriculum Approach 75
B. Curriculum Development and Execution 76

CHAPTER SIX: Program Expectations, Evaluations and Awards ... 91
A. Evaluations 96
B. Rewards 97

CHAPTER SEVEN: Participant Recruitment, Samples of
    Tools Used, and Equipment and Storage 107
A. Recruiting and Selecting CCA Participants............................... 107
B. Samples of Tools Used 111
C. Equipment and Storage... 111

CHAPTER EIGHT: Formal Evaluation of CCA's
    Effectiveness/Success 113
A. Feedback and Awards.. 113
B. Comprehensive Evaluation System.. 116
C. Computerized Database.. 117
D. Comprehensive Evaluation System Reports............................. 118

CHAPTER NINE: Financial Support for Youth Programs 119
A. 2 Million Bullets... 124

CHAPTER TEN: Legal Issues.. 131

CHAPTER ELEVEN: Dealing with the Media 137

APPENDICES 143
A. List of Partners and Sponsors.. 143
B. Reward Types 146
C. Program's Annual Calendar of Events....................................... 148
D. Field Reports and How to Write Them 149
E. Personalized Help for You and/or Your Organization................ 151

ACKNOWLEDGEMENTS

I'd like to acknowledge the many unselfish acts of kindness from others that have allowed my ideas and experiences to become tangibly manifested in this book.

My wife Annette and my son, Landon, deserve gold medals for dealing with my sometimes seemingly silly ideas, my moods, my receipt of many text messages and emails, and the numerous phone calls from others that always seem to creep into our family time.

To my CCA family and my extended family: I owe big hugs to each of you for always believing in our ability to point kids in the right direction, and assisting them in getting to a desirable life destination.

I'd like to thank my "Beyond One Day" team: Chad Groover, Dr. Stanley Ridley, Kathie Sucidlo, and Penny Gage for the important role(s) each played in fostering this book blossoming into printable form.

To my Almighty Father; I humbly continue to help Your youth by using the gifts with which You have blessed me. Thank You for Your favor.

PREFACE

This book is my offering...a way for me to share my passion for helping kids. I was an inner-city kid from a non-typical family, so I know first-hand how important it is for our youth to find positive outlets for their curiosity, energy, and frustrations. My intention here is to relate my experiences as an inner-city youth and to explore the things that helped me evolve into a committed teacher and mentor for youth in similar situations.

I was raised by my grandmother; I didn't know my father, and my mother had issues of her own. I found that I was happiest when I could escape from the city and spend time in the woods adjacent to the housing project where my biological mom lived. I taught myself how to hunt and fish without the advantage of a father or other mentor to guide me. Instead, I looked to other people for the and tools I needed to get started. While I couldn't get away often, just having those activities to look forward to helped me cope with my life situation and kept me away from the negative influences of inner-city living.

Once I got my teaching degree and took a job in an urban middle school in Allentown, Pennsylvania, I knew I wanted to give the students—"my kids"—opportunities to experience the outdoors like I had. I was determined to help them see that there were alternatives to gangs and drugs for their feelings of self-worth, but I wasn't exactly sure how to go about it. I decided to take my personal experiences in hunting, fishing and other outdoor activities and channel them into a framework which eventually evolved into Camp Compass Academy

(CCA). What started as a series of meetings gathered around the "bed" of my truck grew into a multi-award winning non-profit organization with a reputation for helping at-risk youth become constructive, positively contributing adult members of society.

This book is designed to help those of you with a really strong desire to help youth—whether it's your own youth and/or ones at-risk—by either starting your own organization or lending your passion, talent, and energy to an existing organization in your geographical area. I want to reinforce the message that all youth—particularly those in inner-city or urban areas—can benefit greatly from having caring mentors and hands-on conservation, outdoor sports and after-school academic experiences in their lives; and that benefit grows exponentially if they are then given the chance to grow outside the restrictions of the circumstances of their environmental boxes. For this to occur, our involvement with our youth has to go "Beyond One Day."

> If your actions inspire others to
> dream more, learn more,
> do more and become more,
> you are a leader.
>
> **John Quincy Adams**

Instead of seeing our youth for a few hours on a single day, we should spend hours, months, and sometimes years in different situations with them to best foster their adolescent growth.

CHAPTER ONE:
Introduction

A. Today's Youth, Parents or Guardians, and Society

The dynamics of the American family have changed a lot since the end of World War II. The typical family of that era usually had a stay-at-home mother, a father in the labor force, and 2.2 kids. (Still haven't figured out the .2 of a youth.) As parents or guardians pursued the American dream, it became more and more common for both parents or guardians to work. As recently as 2011, in over half of the 2-parent households with youth under the age of 18, both parents or guardians worked—that's a huge familial demographic shift.

Working parents or guardians today are more stressed than in the past. The pressures of an unstable economy, company downsizing/rightsizing, high unemployment rates, ever-increasing prices, and increased demands for their time leave parents or guardians drained and frustrated and their youth starving for adult interaction.

Youth are also subject to some huge stresses that were largely unknown even in the last part of the 20th century. Peer pressure has always been an influencing factor in the lives of adolescents, but technology has opened the door to web sites that encourage things like cheating, sex, and even suicide. Magazines and television commercials eat away at their self-esteem by causing them to question their self-worth, including thinking they're not thin enough, pretty/handsome enough, "cool" enough, or smart enough. Computers and cell phones have opened a whole world of knowledge and socializing that was heretofore inaccessible for most kids. They have also made our kids more vulnerable to bullies and various predators. Physical education courses and recess have all but disappeared from many school systems, and kids would rather surf the net and play video games than take up a sport or participate in varied social and recreational activities, especially ones conducted outdoors.

Urban youth are particularly vulnerable to bad influences in their lives, as their options for taking part in formal and structured outdoor and conservation activities are often woefully limited. Often they are actively solicited by gangs and drug pushers with the promise of easy money and protection from other gangs. Developmentally, youth in middle school and high school can be easily influenced; many are afraid of what the future may bring and what their place in society will be. Gangs promise to make them feel included and show them how to command respect. If that doesn't work, gang leaders may resort to veiled/actual threats by offering to protect the kids and their families from harm. They may go so far as to directly threaten a youth to draw him or her into the gang. These unhealthy influences are responsible for the huge increases we've seen in gang activity over the past five years. For example, according to 2013 statistics on the FBI website, 40% of the more than one million gang members in the US today are under the age of 18. (Also see statistics on the next page.)

Thus, too many of our youth are susceptible to external influences—both bad and good—so getting them involved in a positive program that can help them make good choices in life is essential.

Some Relevant Statistics

- According to a 2011 report by the U.S. Census Bureau, there are 13.7 million single parents or guardians in the United States today.
- 85% of all youth who exhibit behavioral disorders come from fatherless homes (Center for Youth's Justice, 2008).
- According to the 2013 Department of Justice (DOJ) Statistics, 90% of all incarcerated male juveniles have gang affiliations.
- According to an FBI study, gang membership has jumped to 1.4 million since 2009—a 40% increase.
- According to the 2011 US Census, in 57.5% of the 2-parent households with youth under the age of 18, both parents or guardians worked.

Without strong parental influences at home to counterbalance the pressures exerted by the gangs and peer pressure, our youth are in danger of being lost forever. This is the time in their lives when they most need something positive to build their self-esteem. CCA offers youth and their parents or guardians a safe, nurturing alternative to gang membership. We offer a program that will engage them in appealing outdoor activities and teach them that they can be

> "As the [traditional] family unit continues to decline in America, young people are looking for a sense of belonging. For many youths, a gang becomes a new 'family' for them."
>
> **Author Unknown, DOJ 2013**

successful in this world. Their parents or guardians feel secure knowing that their youth are being well-supervised and provided with pertinent life lessons that will help them succeed and that they are kept focused and engaged in a way that will discourage gang and addiction involvement. Our goal is to inspire our youth to seek and achieve a better life.

The toughest part of doing what we do at CCA is where we do it. Crime, gangs, and lack of respect prominent in the inner-city are major factors in why we use America's outdoors, and life lessons they can provide, to help foster our participants' personal, academic and social development.

B. America: Preserving Its Outdoor Sports Traditions/Heritage and Conserving Its Environment

I strongly believe that we need to preserve America's long-standing outdoor sports traditions and heritage. This includes hunting, shooting and fishing; as well as our ongoing need to encourage environmental conservation. I have found that one key way to do that is to appropriately expose our children to each of the preceding for the purpose of fostering their development. This includes aiding them in their transformation into healthy and well-functioning adults who actively participate in, and at the same time, preserve our outdoor sports and conserve our beautiful environment. Those accomplishments can be especially beneficial to urban youth.

Here I'm addressing a group of CCA students. We teamed up with two of our partners, Cabela's and Clover Hollow, for an opportunity to serve youth who had earned the reward of a hunting trip.

Some Relevant Statistics (NY Times, 2010)

- Fewer hunters are involved in the sport each year. For example in Massachusetts there has been a 50 percent decrease in hunting license during the last 20 years.
- In Pennsylvania, license sales have dipped 20 percent over the last two decades. The state's game commission has cut spending by about $1 million in the last two years, cutting back efforts to repopulate pheasants.
- To help stave off outdoor sports participants, some states and outdoor sports groups have increased their efforts to retain and recruit hunters. There has also been an increase in hunting workshops for women and youth.

> Youth need to feel the joy and jubilation of the world; a world that embraces their participation and rewards them with tangible proof of their worth in society. Too often such experiences are inaccessible to inner-city youth.
>
> **John Annoni**

CHAPTER TWO:
Getting Involved With Youth and Programs for Them

A. Finding and Keeping Good People

> "Never underestimate the power of a few committed people to change the world. Indeed, it is the only thing that ever has."
>
> ***Margaret Mead***

I can't stress strongly enough that you have to care—*really care* from within—about youth to make your journey fulfilling. I believe you have to be highly committed to the future of youth before setting a course to get involved. I won't kid you; building an effective organization/program for youth is an exhaustive process that demands commitment, positivity, time, energy, teamwork, patience, and persistence. Whether you're starting a new organization or working to help an existing organization become stronger—the rewards can be huge. You will be lending a hand in developing the character and personal and social abilities of the very people who will soon populate and lead our communities and the world.

An organization is only as good as the people that help it. You already know that, of course, but it's so important that you'll hear me say it again and again. It is essential that you surround yourself with good people—people who are committed, honest, caring, and willing to do whatever it takes to help youth and ensure that programs for them survive and thrive.

In the beginning my effort was like working with modeling clay—as the ideas kept coming and the program grew, I would just add more layers of clay. Most good organizations start from one person's vision, but to bring a program to fruition requires the commitment of many good people. I knew that the only way to attract those good people was to prove to them that I was worthy of their help. No matter what you start out thinking, it always comes back to relationships, trust, and credibility. Bringing in the right people gave me many more resources than I had initially. I knew instinctively that no one person could have all the answers. That was Ken Blanchard's message in his book, High Five. The book was about a boys' hockey team that, despite having lots of star players, still had a losing record. Things turned around as they learned to work together.

When I decided I wanted to help youth, I didn't really have a specific plan for how to get started. I was being driven by a deep-seated desire to provide support and guidance for my students outside the classroom, as well as a gut instinct that I had the aptitude and tools to fill a void. I wasn't too concerned with the trappings of a traditional non-profit—I didn't have a place to meet, I had no money other than my limited savings, and I was the only person on staff. That didn't stop me. I knew I needed to get involved—for "my kids"—and for my community. This wasn't going to be a short-term gesture; it was going to be a long-term commitment. I set a 4-year minimum for myself and the long-term results I wanted to gain. My vision, if I wanted to give it a fair chance of working, would not mature overnight. I wanted to provide a safe outlet for kids to learn about the allure of the outdoors—a concept foreign to many of them—and to show them how to apply the disciplines and skills they learned in nature to common life situations that they would be facing as they transitioned from adolescence to adulthood.

I decided that we were going to work from my mind's eye and use the ideas that I drew on from life sciences, mathematics, language arts and social studies. My goal was to encourage the students to be thoughtful and to use discretion when life brought them face to face with conservation and reality issues. This would be accomplished through the outdoor experiences that would be the basis for the organization. I knew the students would have to be held accountable for their behaviors both in school and on their personal time if they wanted to work with me on this mission of personal growth.

☑ Tips/Reminders

- ☑ Working with kids has to be a labor of love.
- ☑ You must have a passion for helping youth to succeed with them.
- ☑ You must be able to redirect failures.
- ☑ Starting from scratch isn't a short-term activity with participation limited to your spare time; it's a time-consuming, demanding role. If you're unsure of your ability to commit, join an existing organization first to see if you are ready for the challenge. This can be as fully rewarding as starting your own organization.

- ☑ Starting a non-profit doesn't demand a lot of money initially, but fundraising will be an ongoing challenge for continuous and sustainable growth.
- ☑ You will have to prove yourself, your work, and your worth to gain commitments from others.
- ☑ I did all of the work myself at first, but when I finally added others to the staff, I was able to recognize their key attributes and where they could help me with the vision.
- ☑ Stay in contact with students after they leave the program…an alumni group is a valuable resource. The internet and smart phones have made staying in contact an easy task, so get comfortable with email, Facebook, LinkedIn, Twitter, and other social media outlets.
- ☑ To maintain your credibility, do your homework. Be sure you have all the facts and data you need to answer questions that may come your way. If you don't have the answer when a question is posed, say so; then get the answer and promptly follow up with the person that asked the question.
- ☑ Prepare yourself and your helpers to deal with questions. Provide a robust FAQ sheet so that everyone is sharing consistent information about the organization.
- ☑ Recognize that not everyone wants to do more—some are content with their roles. If people ask for more responsibility, assign them roles that feed that need and let them know they are appreciated.

Pitfalls to Avoid

It would be an understatement to say that I made some mistakes along the way. Hopefully, reading about my efforts will help you avoid taking the same missteps.

I didn't do the following:

- Take enough pictures to track the progress and successes of the students and the program in the early years. Remember, there were no digital cameras back then and I had no staff.
- Write a complete business plan and then make tweaks to the initial draft. I needed a living document, and as the program grew, the business plan needed to change and evolve with it.
- Reflect on and celebrate the little successes along the way; I focused too much on big goals, which became discouraging and hurt the momentum of the program.
- Describe my vision succinctly or eloquently enough to attract the number of supporters that I needed.
- Realize that other people might not want to help…even if I was doing the "right thing."

Background Checks

One of the most important requirements for our staff (volunteers, staff and mentors) is a background check—no exceptions. One of the positive aspects of using teachers or others who work with youth in their regular jobs to build a volunteer staff is that these people will have already passed a thorough background check. When we bring on mentors or any other volunteers, background checks are initiated. Our youths' safety is always our first priority. It is absolutely essential that we only work with people with the highest moral and ethical values, and for that reason we take a stand against giving second chances. Although we understand that good people can make mistakes and often deserve another chance, we just don't feel we can accommodate them in our program. We do not consider anyone for a volunteer position working with youth if they have a history of criminal trouble, youth abuse, or addiction. As cold as that sounds, we do everything in our power to focus our energy on the youth and not spend time on the adult's issues. There are, however, opportunities for community service hours that can be completed that don't involve youth; these, in most cases, can also be very fulfilling for those adults.

Beyond background checks, we require that when our mentors are with our kids, they do not smoke, drink, or use profane language. The commitment we ask for is that they will be the upstanding people that we believe they are and that they will be good role models for our kids at all times. We ask that they are open to our system and rely on what our academy represents. Remember the hunting and shooting community has an image in mainstream America, and it's not always that positive when shown in the media. So we do everything we can to prove that the image some people have of beer drinking, "shoot everything up", only for white society—isn't being correctly portrayed. It's a personal, mental and physical commitment for all our volunteers. We hope for an ongoing allegiance from our outreach mentors so that they will have the opportunity to watch the youth and our program grow over time. We ask them to be involved in all aspects of the events they are sponsoring whether it's instructing, skinning a deer or cleaning a shotgun. The commitment we are looking for is that they will take on whatever role is necessary to help the youth achieve his or her mission to accomplish a task and ensure that youth has some sort of personal success.

Events aren't all about hunting and shooting, but they are all about life. For example, getting together and setting goals is healthy.

CHAPTER THREE:
Camp Compass Academy (CCA)

A. The Start

In 1994, I began developing a conservation curriculum that I tested as an after school program for some of my classroom students. The response was strong, and over time my enrichment program became a federally recognized 501(c)(3) organization called Camp Compass Academy (CCA). CCA is a unified program that introduces urban students, grades six through twelve, to a variety of outdoor sports and environmental conservation activities. Students attend classes where they learn about some of the many local and national businesses that offer support for the CCA philosophy (e.g., Cabela's, Bass Pro Shops, Leupold, Mossy Oak and Under Armour). While the program is focused on growing youth through nature and the outdoors, the students are held to a high standard with their school work and behavior as well. CCA is, above all, an elongated learning organization, and students are subject to homework, tests, and evaluations of their experiences. The result has been a population of polite, well-educated young people ready to bring their knowledge and enthusiasm to a cross-section of selected careers, conservation efforts, and sportsmen's activities.

CCA provides urban students the opportunity for hands-on experiences and life lessons designed to broaden their knowledge of the outdoors. They also learn how to apply what they learn in the community at large. Lessons are language-rich so that students are not only learning about the outdoors, but they are also being exposed to grammar, punctuation and vocabulary in an informal manner that demonstrates practical application in everyday situations. The outdoor experiences are infused with language arts, science, social studies and mathematics lessons to enhance learning without the stigma of a "boring classroom" attached. CCA's incremented program dispels many of the myths about sportsmen and conservation and allows students to use their personal discretion when making judgments about conservation and firearms-related issues. CCA is composed of five stages: Exposure, Exploration, Extension, Effective Application, and Example Mentoring. Each stage prepares students to move up to the next level in the program. All levels have specifically adapted features designed to enhance the CCA educational agenda. The program's philosophy goes "BEYOND ONE DAY" at an event, in the woods or on the water, and it has given students a new outlook on conservation, sportspersons' philosophies and life. I founded a program that links different cultures, ages and socioeconomic groups to ensure that our country's great outdoor sports heritage continues to progress into the future.

> "Vision without action is a daydream.
> Action without vision is a nightmare."
>
> **Japanese Proverb**

Some old school shirts our students used to wear "back in the day"—as their CCA uniform tops. Thanks Mossy Oak, for making these available.

The major reason I started CCA was because I wanted to do something for youth above and beyond the classroom. The academy space wasn't actually part of my original vision.

I never once consciously thought, "Hey, I'm going into business." I didn't have a solid business plan or a host of investors with deep pockets ready to buy equipment or pay for hunting trips, but I was now making a living teaching, and I wanted to reinvest some of the dollars I made into helping my students beyond the four walls of my classroom. I knew that I loved the outdoors—that hunting and fishing and being in the outdoors had been my refuge from a really trying childhood—and I was totally committed to finding a way to share those passions with youth.

My first meetings were held around the back hatch of my truck. The trips we took were trips that I would have taken anyway—so why not take a few kids along with me? I would always think that way. We visited fish hatcheries and game preserves on the money I had left over from my teacher's salary at the end of the month.

Yes, I funded those first meetings out of my savings and whatever I could eke out of my paycheck. When I finally realized I needed some actual startup money, I borrowed from my son's bank account. Now as you can imagine, this didn't go over really well with my wife, but I promised her that he would eventually get it all back. I knew that my son was going to be okay because he was still small. I would keep putting a little money away out of my paycheck, and I would just use his money until my program got established. I knew that I needed to help more kids than I could finance on my meager savings alone, and this was the only way I could see to put my passion into play.

Needless to say, I've learned a lot since those days. CCA is now a 501(c)(3) nonprofit, but in the beginning, I wasn't even sure what a non-profit encompassed. Frankly, I had no idea what a 501(c)(3) even was.

When I first started trying to find the money to fund my efforts to help youth, I made a lot of mistakes. I had heard of local groups that were giving money away to "help the community," so I just walked into a local trust office and said, "Hey, I'm John Annoni. I'm a teacher, and I'm trying to help kids. What do I need to do to get some help?" The woman behind the desk asked if the organization was a 501(c)(3). I bet the look on my face said it all. It was probably the same look you give someone when you're trying to understand a foreign language. Then she asked if we were a charity. I wasn't sure how to answer that, so I asked her what she meant. She explained the criteria for charity status, and I had to say no. It was pretty embarrassing that I didn't know the lingo, but I'll never apologize for my passion for helping kids. Needless to say, I didn't get the money…but shortly after, I met a great guy at a hunting lodge while hunting with a student he thought was my daughter. I clarified what we were doing at the lodge. I told him my story and how I'd bungled my attempt to secure a trust donation to move my ideas forward, and by the grace of God, he offered to help me get established as a 501(c)(3)…I'm convinced that was Divine Intervention.

CCA was now a paper reality instead of just a vision. It was designed to introduce urban middle and high school students to the excitement, adventure, and the many activities that can be enjoyed in the outdoors. Our students are prepared to face real world situations. We help them increase their self-esteem, give them role models to help them build character and encourage them to make solid, positive choices in their lives.

Since the program started in 1994, our volunteers have mentored and developed many thousands of youth. Our programs, built around American heritage outdoor sports like hunting, shooting, fishing, archery, camping, etc., have proven their value over and over again to the students, the parents or guardians, and the community. Our volunteer mentors make a real difference in the lives of our kids. They give freely of their time, energy, enthusiasm and creativity, and through them, this unique, elongated program has become the most successful of its kind in the nation.

> "Challenges can be stepping stones or stumbling blocks. It is a matter of how you view them."
>
> **Author Unknown**

CHAPTER THREE 35

We provide CCA participants individualized adult support for academics and outdoor sports adventures.

Think girls aren't interested in outdoor sports, and can't be successful doing them?—WRONG!

B. Who We Are and What We Do

Before I started CCA, I had to think long and hard about what it was that I wanted. I certainly wasn't looking at the business side of the program. My focus was on finding my students a place where they felt safe—even safer than they felt in school—a place where they could be themselves, learn about themselves, and see and do things that they had never dreamed were possible. Most of all, I wanted to help them prepare for successful lives.

We manage CCA very well with a surprisingly small staff. We have only three paid part-time positions; otherwise, the program is run completely by committed volunteers and with the help of our sponsors and donors.

The CCA philosophies are simple. We believe the following:

- The CCA staff is being called on to use our passions to help the next generation bring a new-found healthy quality to their lives.
- Every youth, no matter what his/her circumstances, should have the opportunity to experience positive people and activities in their daily lives.
- We provide the bridge for our students so they can spend time in the field, and on the water.
- In today's tough environment, we—as adults, must—provide not only advice, but a ready ear for listening as well.
- Kids are the key to our success. We change the lives of the youth we touch and that motivates us to do more.
- We can't save every youth, but we have devised a unique system that allows us to touch and impact lives deeply.

- As we usher the youth that will benefit the most through our progressive efforts, we are able to become involved with them over a period of years.

My expectations for CCA and what it should be were extremely high. For me, it was like going on vacation and staying at a really nice hotel: I knew that I would be paying more for the room, but if it met my expectations, I didn't mind paying the price—I got what I paid for. The stakes are just as high for America's youth. When a youth says that he or she likes spending time with you, it is both humbling and an honor. If more people that are influenced by the outdoors were willing to give back in the truest sense of the word (and not just offer lip service), we could alter the direction being taken by a lot of our youth today and improve the image and declining numbers of sportsmen and women.

C. Personnel/Shareholders and Their Roles and Responsibilities

There are basically six groups of people that contribute to the overwhelming success of CCA:

1. Board of Directors and Advisors
2. Executives/Manager
3. Staff
4. Volunteers
5. Mentors
6. Sponsors, Donors and Partners

Board of Directors (BOD) and Advisors.

CCA has five-member BOD. All members have expertise in education and youth development. Their roles are consistent with those of traditional BODs. The Advisors are individuals that provide strategic advice to our organization. Both I and CCA benefit from the worldly knowledge of our advisors.

Let's briefly look at each of the other groups more closely.

Executives/Manager

I act as the CCA Executive Director; my wife, as the Executive Secretary; works closely with me (we found out rather quickly due to the schedule I'm on that a traditional secretary would not work). We have an extremely talented individual managing our volunteer staff. He also handles the logistics for our trips and our outdoor experiences.

Initially, and for many years, these were non-paid positions, quite simply because there was no money for payroll, and we all wanted to make sure the program survived. Now, 20 years later, we are able to provide minimal compensation for these positions.

Our organization has never been about individuals making a lot of money—if we actually paid salaries commensurate with effort and involvement, it would break a few banks.

Staff Volunteers and Mentors

We rely on three different categories of support staff:
1. Educational Volunteers
2. Outreach Mentors
3. Fundraising Volunteers

These individuals collectively donate thousands of hours of service, classroom training and field hours each year. All of our volunteers are vital members of our team but each has a slightly different role.

Educational Volunteers

These individuals have backgrounds in education. They work directly with the youth and are comprised mostly of teachers and/or people with an educational perspective. They work at the academy's physical space. We are able to provide a small stipend for these educational volunteers, via grants, so they can prepare and purchase materials for the youth to use in classes. The commitment they make is often 3-7 volunteer hours a week during the school year. Many people might say that giving that much time is impossible, but I say that some of society's problems have escalated because too few people are willing to commit the necessary hours to guide youth. Yes, even some parents or guardians don't give the amount of time our EV's do. If we truly care about America's kids and its future, we should be willing to do whatever it takes to put them firmly on a path to success.

Educational Volunteers are a critical factor in CCA's success. Their contributions have included providing a constant physical presence while also ensuring consistency in the quality of our academic offerings.

Outreach Mentors

An additional and essential component of our volunteer staff is our outreach mentors that work with us in the field. These are the folks who have particular skills that they can bring to the program. For us, it might be someone who is an experienced deer hunter, and is willing to help us take a group of kids on a deer hunt. Or perhaps there is someone with experience hunting in Africa—this person could give a presentation to larger groups about his/her experience hunting big game in another country. Outreach mentors do not work with the kids as frequently as our academy staff, but they are well-versed in a wide range of diverse topics that we want to cover with the kids, and they are willing to share their knowledge and expertise with us when they are needed. We have found that our greatest success stories have one thing in common—they started with a partnership between an outreach mentor and an educational volunteer. They work as a tag team, with the outreach mentors bringing their expertise to the task at hand, and the academy volunteers taking physical responsibility for the kids. If the educational volunteer is also well-versed in the topic being studied, so much the better, because that's when we hit a home run and our rewards become that much more meaningful for all involved - even the adults.

Our Outreach Mentors aid CCA and society by sharing their passion and expertise with outdoor sports so that our kids stay excited and engaged when participating.

Fundraising Volunteers

Without fundraising, CCA couldn't survive. Our Fund Raiser Volunteers not only help with our funding, their ideas and energy serve our mission well. The best thing about their work is that it helps youth.

Fund raising is a never-ending consideration for an organization like ours. We are a 501(c)(3) nonprofit, and the need for funds to run our programs is constant and ongoing. We have never received government support. However, we have a group of volunteers focused on trying to secure funds from various means. I play the biggest part in that because of my role as Executive Director. Without the efforts of people setting up, tearing down, and searching for opportunities, we would not be able to keep our vital efforts going. We have been tremendously fortunate that our fund-raising volunteers have been overly cautious handling money. There is always a risk that cash might disappear. Setting up a PayPal account, a bank account and a system of checks and balances for donors is your best bet to begin. Use common sense and make sure that you ask your volunteers to get a name and contact information for all cash contributions.

We provide as-needed training for our volunteers, as well as a checklist for everyone to consider when filling his or her roles. Some of the components of the checklist may seem very basic, but we try to balance the structure of the program with hands-on opportunities so volunteers aren't bored to death with paperwork or classroom sitting.

☑ Tips/Reminders

Volunteers should
- ☑ Not use cell phones for calls or texting while driving. If a call is necessary, do so when you have stopped the car (e.g., when you stop to eat or buy gas) and when you are on non-student engaged time.

- ☑ Be aware of how much time you will have to commit to an event before the onset of a trip. Nothing is more upsetting to continuity and to all involved than if you forgot you had something else to attend to and need to leave early, especially on non-controllable events that can be impacted by weather and/or animal movement.
- ☑ Make sure the vehicle being driven has been inspected and is in good working condition—not only do you need to have a spare tire, but you need a jack as well! Road service is only good if you have cell service, so know your plan for breakdowns (this is especially important in cold weather).
- ☑ Be aware of bathroom situations—places where you can stop, making sure that no one goes to the bathroom alone, what kinds of facilities will be available at the destination, etc. This is especially critical to female participants. Just because you may feel comfortable peeing behind a tree, doesn't make it "normal."
- ☑ Know if any of the youth have allergies, what they are, what kinds of medications are needed and where the closest medical facility is.
- ☑ Be prepared with the appropriate clothing required for the trip being taken. Check the forecast and believe in it. If it says slight chance of rain and you decide not to bring rain gear, it will pour. PLAN! If a formal educational facility closes due to weather, use their decision to guide the cancellation or postponement of a trip. Use professionals to help you make good decisions; don't rely on a "4-wheel drive" mentality.

Ensuring our CCA particpants have appropriate clothing and equipment is a key to maximizing the positive experiences available when engaing in outodoor sports. Having the needed clothing and equipment can prevent Mother Nature from robbing us of wonderful opportunities—Actually, sometimes a little water makes the day that much more memorable!

We shoot a variety of calibers of rifles and shotguns, but our safety expectations are the same for each.

- Be sure (when going on a shooting or hunting trip) that you know what guns the kids will be using and that both you and the mentors are well versed and comfortable with the firearms for that event. At CCA we have a unified system for our firearms so the guns our students train on are the ones they use in the field. It cuts out a lot of the unknown issues and allows both the student and mentor to focus on the experience beyond the gun.

More on Volunteering

Three C's for Successful Volunteers:

Confidentiality - Exercise discretion in matters relating to student learning and behaviors. Comments and concerns, if any, are to be shared only with the academy staff. Volunteers must respect the privacy of others by avoiding inappropriate comments about students or staff members. It is inappropriate to discuss the personal information of a student or staff member with a third party.

Concern – Demonstrate a caring, positive attitude at all times. Students recognize and thrive on genuine encouragement.

Compatibility – Foster mutual respect and understanding for the roles and responsibilities of the academy staff and volunteers. In doing so, you facilitate trust between the volunteers and academy staff.

Expectations:

Before working solo with CCA Students, all volunteers are required to:
Submit a completed application form
Pass a criminal background check
Obtain a youth child abuse clearance

While working with Academy students:

- Absolutely no tobacco products, alcohol or illegal substances are permitted.
- All volunteers are required to sign-in when they arrive at the academy or an event, and sign-out when they leave.
- Do not leave personal items (e.g., purses, briefcases, etc.) unattended. Leave these items at home, in your car, or at the office.
- Never use cell phones while transporting students. (This was worth mentioning again!) If you must use the phone, pull off the road until the call is completed.
- Please contact the parents or guardians as a courtesy if you are transporting students and you will be more than 20 minutes late returning from an event.
- You will be briefed on your specific roles and the expectations for the day/event when traveling with students.
- Student needs must come first in every situation.
- Have fun while meeting job expectations.
- Evaluate all student outings they attend.

Sponsors, Partners and Donors

Your sponsors, community partners and donors can make a huge difference in the effectiveness of your organization. The people and business supporters you seek out will depend on the nature of your program's mission. For our program, we look for those organizations, businesses and individuals that are involved with or value shooting and hunting. We collaborate with them in many different ways. Businesses like Cabela's and other similar local businesses in the outdoor industry are willing to let us bring our kids in for field trips. While there, we call on the store staff to supplement our students' knowledge about hunting, shooting, choosing the proper equipment for different kinds of outings, and safety. This is all pre-planned, of course, and is a great example of outreach mentoring. These special outings provide a safe initial exposure for our kids who might otherwise not even have been comfortable walking into the store. Don't be surprised if after one of these field trips your kids take their families right back to that very same establishment and begin to introduce them to what they learned. If a kid is made to feel comfortable, exponential growth CAN happen. One last thing: when out and about, let the kids take pictures with their phones and then share them. Nothing shows kids having fun and relieves their parents or guardians' skepticism like happy photos of their youth actually learning something.

No one can argue about whether our kids smiling has an impact on us—it does, tremendously!

CCA's inclusion of our Partners undoubtedly makes a positive impact on all involved; we know well the validity of this statement: "Together Everyone Achieves More."

CCA participants fully engaged? Yes, they are, and we love it!

> Donors don't give to institutions. They invest in ideas and people in whom they believe.
>
> ## G.T. Smith

When you are looking for sponsors, partners, and donors the first step is to identify those that align with your values. These are the individuals or groups you'll want to approach for support. Keep in mind that support comes in many forms besides money. At CCA, we look to outdoor businesses, gun clubs and shooting ranges for support. They are perfect partners for us. We have a partnership with one of the best sporting clay shooting facilities in the country, Lehigh Valley

Sporting Clays. They offer us not only shooting opportunities but also an atmosphere of class our youth sometimes lack. At some of the local gun clubs, we can take advantage of the one-day events they offer throughout the year to provide outings for our kids that are in the extension and exploration phases of our program.

Lehigh Valley Sporting Clays is CCA's home for shotgun training. That entity not only provides a place for us to shoot, but its first-class facilities and environment yields yet another type of very positive experience in our participants' lives that many of them would otherwise probably never have.

CHAPTER THREE 53

Pictured above are the guys that gave me my first chance—Toxey Haas (L) and Ronnie Strickland (R) from our Partner, Mossy Oak. Because of our shared caring for youth, our relationship with that company has lasted 20 years. Below is one of the many pieces of equipment our Partners like Alps OutdoorZ have donated for our CCA participants to use so they can learn about and enjoy outdoor sports.

We look for contributions from our sponsors, partners, and donors in the form of money, products, and/or services. We learned, however, that to get a sponsor's or a partner's attention, we first had to prove that our organization and/or mission was worthy of their support; and this is done through networking, contacts, and time.

Obviously you won't be the only person and organization looking for support. You'll have to show that your program is unique and worth their time, energy, and contributions. You can't do that unless you make a concerted effort to remain in contact with members of these groups. Make no mistake! This is hard work, and it takes time, but to get started you need to grab any opportunity you can, wherever you can. That means you go to trade shows and attend dinners sponsored by local businesses and organizations, volunteer to do presentations, or offer to explain your organization to a local radio personality. Try anything that will make people more aware of the value of your program's philosophy, mission, and how it benefits for youth and the community.

☑ Tips/Reminders

- ☑ Don't hesitate to ask questions; jump at any chance to explain your mission.
- ☑ Tell anyone that will listen how you will help kids.
- ☑ Point out how the sponsor or partner can benefit by becoming part of your team.
- ☑ Do not "disgrace" the value of the donor's product. They want you to get the most you can for their product or service.

Once you have made your contacts, let potential sponsors know that they may be able to write off their contributions of products or services if you are a designated 501(c)(3) non-profit organization. We often ask lodge owners to donate a free night of lodging for our reward trips. Many of these potential sponsors have excess products they may have overstocked or products they are taking out of their inventory that they would be happy to donate. Your task is to figure out a way to turn that excess product into capital or incentives for your organization and volunteers. If allowed by law, you might run a raffle or collect donations for their donated equipment at a flea market or in an on-line auction. You can tell the sponsor that you will gladly use their name to make sure they

> We make a living by what we get.
> We make a life by what we give.
>
> **Winston Churchill**

get positive publicity for their donation. One word of caution: keep the lines of communication open with the product donors so that they know exactly how their product is being used.

It's really important that you express your gratitude when a donation is made to your program—regardless of the value or size of the support. Further, never underestimate the impact of a hand-written thank you note. This is a dying art in our society today, and it can really set your organization apart from all the others. Many times we have our kids write our thank you notes; the sponsors are impressed with the efforts the kids are taking to write the notes, and the notes provide yet another learning, branding, and social opportunity for our students.

So we're full circle—to get good people you have to make contacts; you have to be willing to work hard, to be seen, and to be approachable; and you have to be willing to effectively use the support people can offer. It is your responsibility, goal, and obligation to figure out how to make what they have to offer work for your organization.

Good people and quality clothing and sports products help the CCA program succeed!

Some Relevant Statistics

- Approximately one in four Americans volunteer. People that volunteer are almost twice as likely to donate to charities as people that don't volunteer (Corp. for National and Community Services).

- According to the Bureau of Labor Statistics, the volunteer rate in 2013 was the lowest it has been since it was first measured in 2002.
- 64.5 million Americans volunteered 7.9 billion hours in 2013. Those hours have an estimated value of $175 billion (Corp. For National and Community Services).
- According to a report by Volunteer Management, only 35% of all non-profits recognize the contributions of their volunteers, and only 45% of those non-profits match volunteers' skills with appropriate assignments.

Pitfalls to Avoid

- Don't choose your associates based solely on their alignment with your interests. It is critical to bring many different talents and perspectives to your table to balance the expertise.
- When you are trying to make contacts, avoid doing so when you might have over-indulged in a little too much alcohol. Remember, you are always representing yourself, your organization—your brand. Maintaining your credibility and keeping your reputation impeccable are crucial if you want people to align with your mission and acknowledge what you have accomplished in the community. I'm not saying you can't ever let loose, but use discretion when you want to conduct business.
- Don't just choose people who understand and share your passion. For example, not having financial experts delayed our progress. Lack of balance and pressure on individuals to wear many hats can be exhausting if you don't pace yourself and your team.

☑ Tips/Reminders

- ☑ Examine your individual organizational structure to determine if and how much you can pay your workers. I suggest you start with as many volunteers as possible; then allow your volunteers to earn paid staff positions when they become available. The priority is to find volunteers that are as committed to the mission as you are. If things go well, in time you should be able to compensate your top people —those that created the momentum for success.
- ☑ Use your volunteers carefully to fully maximize their effectiveness. Know what their strengths are and take the time necessary to match them to appropriate assignments. If you are the volunteer, expect your leadership to act similarly.
- ☑ To avoid volunteer burnout, keep your volunteers positioned on annual teams for specific events and rewards. Don't overuse them to the point of abuse unless they "love" the abuse. Most volunteers go full-throttle when they first join an organization—they want to see progress and feel valued. Be careful not to let them over-do, or their flames may burn out far too soon.
- ☑ Value your volunteers and make sure they know how much they are appreciated. Your organization couldn't exist without them. In this busy world THANK YOU means a lot.
- ☑ If you don't have enough volunteers or staff to cover all the work that needs to be done, there are websites that can provide various services for a nominal fee. Since we don't have a full time employees work at CCA, we rely on a site called FIVERR.com to bridge gaps in our staff

A hand-written thank you card with a picture of the event and/or the youth doing an activity can be very special for the adults who participated. Sure it takes a little effort, but CCA participants enjoy doing it; and, we've found that doing so is always much appreciated by the recipients.

—for example, we use their experts for graphics, social media and to proof read and evaluate certain materials.
- ☑ Make an effort to find volunteers fluent in a second language—this can be invaluable as your organization grows. Bilingual parents or guardians are an excellent resource when trying to convey what the program is about and for keeping others apprised of what is happening with the program.
- ☑ Allow potential volunteers, donors and sponsors to get to know the real you. If you're in alignment, great. If you're not, let them go. I found that when I started, I wasted far too much time trying to convince people that either didn't need convincing or that could never be convinced to help us. You only have so much time, so use it wisely.

- ☑ Spend the money needed for business cards with your logo and an identifying tag line. We use Vistaprint.com. Carry them with you at all times and hand them out to anyone who shows even the slightest interest in you, your vision, or your program. Keeping your name in front of people can lead to big opportunities when they are making decisions to help youth.
- ☑ When looking for volunteers and/or sponsors, never let a "no" discourage you. Keep asking and casting, knowing that what you are doing is important and well worth the effort. The pain of 10 rejections is healed with one "yes."
- ☑ Lead by example. When your staff sees you doing "grunt work," it relays a powerful message about the focus you have. "Cleaning toilets" will keep you grounded and make you appreciate how far you have come.
- ☑ Promote your staff (paid and unpaid) and assign roles based on merit. Take time to ensure that the person potentially selected for a position is qualified and willing to make the commitment required of the position before you move your plans forward.
- ☑ Do background checks. You are working with youth and their mental and physical safety is your primary concern. You can complete background checks for your state online. Don't assign volunteers to work with youth alone until they have been cleared. No exceptions. If the volunteer's place of employment can provide written proof that a background check has been verified, a follow up call will confirm it.

CHAPTER FOUR:
CCA Program Goals, Stages, and Special Emphases

A. Specific Program Goals

The specific CCA program goals are cited below.

- Continue to help students in urban underserved areas develop both culturally, socially and academically.
- Allow interaction between youth, adults and businesses beyond the traditional classroom.
- Integrate adaptive Science, Math, Social Studies and English into outdoor sports and conservation activities.
- Develop character and self-esteem through student-centered learning.
- Build bridges between cultures, ages and socioeconomic status.
- Demonstrate conservation practices and environmental respect through outdoor sports with an emphasis on hunting and shooting.
- Promote a positive connection with the community.
- Offers community job links and student references.
- Take a proactive approach toward firearm safety and education.
- Give outdoor sports, with an emphasis on hunting and shooting, a chance to expand its clientele.

B. Program's Five Stages

At its inception, CCA (unnamed at that point) was divided into 4 distinct levels. It was going to be a learning organization with students advancing based on time invested, use of skills, and knowledge gained through lessons and hands-on outdoor activities. The nature of the program would strengthen relationships between everyone involved. The graphic below (Fig. 1) offers a snapshot of the *current* cyclical progression that the program levels of the organization take. Note: The 5th step was added about 10 years ago to allow older students the opportunity to give back to the program. (With slight, but important word changes to the last two stages, last year the five stages were nicknamed the "five E's".)

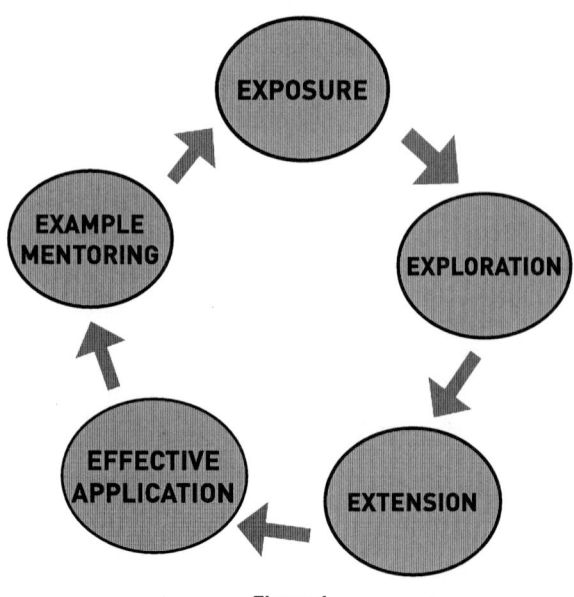

Figure 1

Exposure – The initial stage of the program—this is where the vision for the program and expectations are shared. The level is exactly what the name implies—a time for participants to be exposed to what we have to offer and for them to decide if there are opportunities that interest them.

Exploration – This level allows the students and their custodial adults to take a closer look at the topics and activities that captured their attention during Exposure. During this level, participants explore more directly and intensely the program's offerings. This level includes things like youth field days, trade shows and one-day mass youth events.

Extension – This level offers participants the opportunity to organize their goals. This is where they start to match the topics/activities offered to their own personalities. During Extension, students agree to invest the time needed to prepare socially, mentally, physically and academically for the Effective Application level. Extension is where the organization really earns the trust and respect of the youth and his or her family.

Effective Application – Students draw on the knowledge and skills gained in the previous levels and participate in outdoor events and activities e.g., hunting, fishing & competitive shooting, that challenge their abilities. This stage encourages youth to express their diverse thoughts and feelings in a safe environment. These opportunities—led by experienced adults—are carefully orchestrated "rewards." They are designed to help the students cope with the challenges they will face as they approach adulthood. Over the course of the event they will have to make decisions on their own, apply appropriate social skills, participate in mission planning, demonstrate responsibility, and validate their integrity. They will celebrate their successes and learn from their mistakes. These events are, most often, life-altering for participants and are an integral part of learning to be productive members of the program and the community in which they live. This stage offers rewards for the commitment we have all given to meeting set program goals.

Example Mentoring – The final phase of the program. Only a handful of the students opt to pursue this stage. This is the "Pay It Forward" level of the program. Older students are coached on how to guide, support, listen, and reinforce healthy behaviors in their younger peers. Youth that enter this stage help perpetuate the program while providing real-life examples of what the program can accomplish for the younger students. Their involvement helps us reduce the convincing we have to do. They are living proof of not only our successes but of the tangible results from which lower level students can draw. At the same time, our mentoring-level students continue to acquire additional skills that will help them grow into stronger, more compassionate adults.

> "You don't understand anything until you learn it more than one way."
>
> **Marvin Minsky, American Scientist**

The real advantage of the mentoring level is that it provides the most effective way to ensure that lessons have been learned: we ask the student to become the teacher or role model. Once they can successfully share what they learned in the previous levels, we can be sure they have committed their lessons to long-term memory and will have the skills and knowledge acquired at CCA at their disposal for life.

CHAPTER FOUR 65

We had to add a mentoring level to CCA because a number of our graduates wanted to give back to our program.

Example Mentors have taken the CCA journey and, recognizing its value, wanted to give something back.

C. Special Program Emphases

Preparing Youth for the "Real World"

So how can the millions of people across the United States that hunt and kill animals purport to love nature? Conservation and sound management principles can answer that question. However, most city people don't often think about it as an immediate youth concern. There are a lot of issues facing the kids in America today, and developing a love of nature can help them understand, cope with, and resolve some of those issues. They need to establish a relationship with Mother Nature. Do they all have to kill something to form that relationship? No, but most of the youth that we deal with do need to have a true understanding and love of nature and recognize how it models life and death. In the city, where we primarily do our work, kids die every day. We want our kids to realize how quickly something can change. For example, if a kid is sitting in a tree stand and a deer walks out, he has to make a conscious decision to end its life. That youth knows that once he pulls the trigger and the bullet hits a vital organ, which is the goal, that deer's life is over in a matter of seconds. The deer was in the wrong place at the wrong time. It's a life lesson, but one every kid—particularly a city kid—needs to know and become intimate with.

People who are unfamiliar with who we are as hunters or fishermen—conservationists—don't necessarily see how these lessons in the field relate to the kids' lives. We need to help them understand that the strong kids are going to get the good jobs, and the weak ones will struggle. There are only a limited number of jobs available at any given time, and once they're taken, what happens to those kids that didn't make the cut?

In the field, the kids learn that the stronger deer survive. It may be because they're nocturnal or that they're smart… Mother Nature gives deer a sixth sense, a reflex or instinct to survive. When a kid develops that instinct to survive in the real world of jobs and competition, he or she often does pretty well.

We teach our kids respect for the animals they hunt and respect for themselves. Once a kid learns respect—once he stands over a deer that he shot, his natural curiosity sets in. He naturally wants to explore that critter even more. He wants to look at the organs, to see if he hit the heart (an interesting point is that our middle school girls are much more interested in this part than the boys). I know that sounds a little crazy, but it is part of what our kids take with them—an understanding of how the body works. We discuss the mistakes the deer made and how those same mistakes might crop up in our daily lives. For the kid that has a missed shot, he may turn to his volunteer and/or mentor and say, "Hey, my heart is pumping." That opens the door for a conversation about adrenaline and the effects it has on the body and mind.

Primarily, the shooting, hunting, and fishing that we embrace are teaching kids that there are rules to the game of life and death. We show them that when they follow the rules and respect Mother Nature for who she is and what she provides, they'll end up respecting life that much more. Their love of nature will then grow to include their homes and families. When the youth bring home meat for the family table or donate it to the local food bank they become providers—roles they will play for their rest of their lives once they have families of their own.

CCA graduates with their own families.

CHAPTER FOUR 69

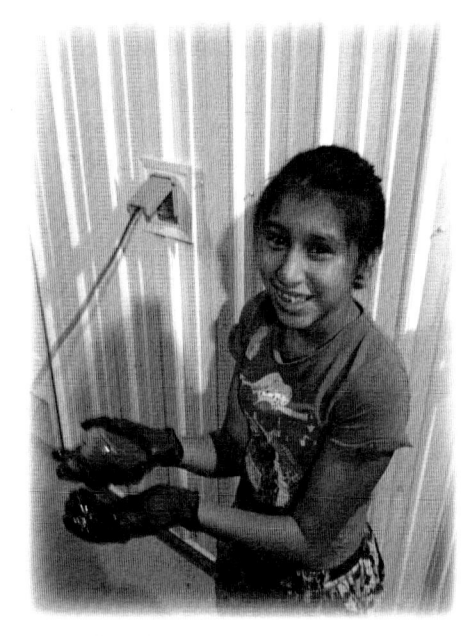

Youth are naturally curious, and we capitalize on that curiosity. In these pictures, one can see examples of how CCA helps relate book lessons about biology, anatomy, measurement and accuracy to real life. Above, a student studies a heart, and below, shot placement is displayed by the girls who participated in an evening hunt.

People sometimes ask us if we take our kids hiking, and we respond that we "hike up the mountain to hunt game." Our kids develop a love for Mother Nature. They take from her, and then give back by wanting to help her. I think that's what a lot of mainstream Americans don't understand about CCA or hunters in general. I respect that anti-hunters want to save God's creatures, but we're trying to save God's most important creatures—our youth. My sincere hope, when I see the millions of dollars that are donated annually to hunting and shooting charities across America, is that more donors will see the value of investing those hard-earned contributions in our youth and the people who help them grow. Our kids are our future, and the future of hunting and shooting. The smart money needs to support that future if what we love is to survive.

Making it Personal

Anyone that wants to work with youth and in the same breath says that he or she can't get involved in their personal lives needs to rethink his commitment. With kids, it has to get personal. Trying to maintain a "little distance" over time may create a chasm that can't be repaired. Kids are very intuitive, and if they feel you aren't committed to them 100%, they can read all kinds of interpretations into the why of it. You may think you're staying impartial and not intruding in their lives, but they may think you're being aloof—that they aren't good enough, or smart enough, or important enough for you to care about them. The bottom line is, you have to be there not just on meeting day or for events but anytime they need you. You have to be on time. You have to commit. You have to care.

CHAPTER FOUR

Hey, Zachi, I miss you. Thanks for taking me turkey hunting. Check it out on YouTube @ Zachi Goes Turkey Hunting. Zachi passed away from cancer, but no one taught me more about the little things in life than him. I hope this book includes some little things that will contribute to making the quality of your life better too.

Diversity

In the dictionary, diverse is defined as "of a different kind, form, or character." Without diversity, there would be no spice to life. The kids that I work with are the very definition of diverse. They come from different ethnic, financial, familial, and religious backgrounds. While CCA primarily focuses on urban and under-served adolescents, it is open to any youth that needs our help. Part of our work is helping students recognize and learn to appreciate the differences in others and find ways to work together. By cultivating respect and acceptance through the common goals and achievements that are inherent to our heritage of hunting and shooting, they are building a foundation for a more compassionate and unified world.

We pride ourselves in our approach to diversity.

America's hunting and shooting heritage may eventually come to an end if we don't bring in new people who are interested in participating in such outdoor sports. Efforts to do so might mean making some current participants a little uncomfortable. Typically, The issue should not be about race or religion; the focus should be about recruiting anyone who is likely to do a good job carrying the torch for our outdoor sports heritage.

CHAPTER FIVE:
Curriculum Approach, Development and Execution

A. Curriculum Approach

CCA, as the name implies, is about more than just the exposure to and benefits of our country's heritage of outdoor activities like shooting and hunting. There is a large academic component involved as well. The educational volunteers devote a great deal of time looking for ways to help the kids improve their academic skills using the outdoors as a focus. Our students have to earn the right to go on reward trips, and working towards good grades in school is an important requirement. That doesn't mean our students have to earn all A's. There are so many variables that aren't seen on a report card that it's unfair to compare student grades to each other or even against the traditional grading system. Our educational volunteers work with our students on their school assignments and the assignments we give them. The adults read the kids' report cards to spot trends and determine where additional help may be necessary. They also incorporate many learning techniques in their work that may not be readily apparent to the kids. An example of how they do this is by working cognitive thinking into discussions about shooting with a bow and arrow—the kids are focused on the excitement of shooting and don't consciously realize they are also learning about wind, the speed of the arrow, the arc or trajectory needed to hit the bulls eye, etc.

A CCA participant's raised hand means "engagement" and that's what we need to encourage in today's youth in a lot of appropriate contexts.

B. Curriculum Development and Execution

The curriculum at CCA is unique for a number of reasons. We combine traditional instruction in subjects like math, social studies, science and good manners with more modern interactions such as business networking, internet safety and public speaking and then seamlessly intermingle them with our American heritage sports of shooting, hunting, and fishing. By making the topics both fun and functional, the learning is painless and relatable. It's really not as hard as it sounds but does take a bit of training.

When I began to think about a curriculum, I had to reflect back on my childhood and how important it was for me to be able to get away from dangerous and stressful situations at home. The water and the woods were my refuge—they helped me survive. Getting to the peace and safety of the woods was like crossing a bridge...there was this kid living on one side of the bridge and on the other side were the water and the woods. The journey across that bridge helped too. It wasn't *just* about being in the woods like some people thought. It was the journey to get there, too. If I was going hunting or fishing, I had a lot of preparation just to get ready to go. Then there was the anticipation, the waiting, which actually helped me manage the time I had to wait for the day or hunt to arrive.

I want people to start paying more attention to that bridge the kids have to cross to get to an event, and that leads back to what I call multi-mission mentoring. We allow our kids to travel the bridge and get to the other side, because that's what helps them get through life. If you look at our overall program, getting our kids across that opportunity bridge is an extension of their growth; it gives them opportunities to anticipate and then do things that will help them have happier childhoods. Once they get to the woods and water, Mother Nature takes over and what she gives them is intangible...it's internalized. Yes, the woods and water makes them feel better, but it's the journey to get to the woods and water that makes this a life-changing process. The peace and safety of the woods help define kids, but the journey is the real accomplishment.

The chance to be successful—whether catching a fish or bagging a pheasant—is a bonus; the feelings of peace and safety come from the actions the volunteers and Mother Nature have put in motion. We build trust into our program at every opportunity. Think about this: you wouldn't send a kid to the store alone if he had to walk through dangerous dark alleys, would you? That's what a lot of programs do. They expect youth to take on new experiences without fear. Instead, a volunteer walks with the youth, letting him know that there is someone right beside him the entire time. That builds a strong bond between the volunteer and the youth and models safety, love and attention.

We want our trips to be reasonably stress-free for the kids. Adolescents deal with enough stress in their daily lives. We let the adults deal with the stress. When on reward trips, we don't want the kids bothered by extrinsic things like sirens and horns and people yelling at each other…these daily stressors can take a toll on youth development. The woods are serene. Here the kids can listen to themselves…listen to their consciences, to their inner selves. It allows them to know that their decision-making processes are valid and gives them the opportunity to grow from the inside out. It encourages them to use all five senses where typically their senses are stifled in a lot of their day-to-day situations.

When we talk about the peace and safety of the woods and the water, it's important to look at the whole journey. The student going on a reward trip has to think about how to dress for the terrain he'll be on, he has to figure out what ammunition he will need for the game he's pursuing, and he has to get up on time so he can eat a good breakfast and double check his gear before he leaves the lodge. All of these little details are going to be stored away in his memories about this day so that when things get tough or he has to prepare again, he can draw on the prior experiences to help him pull through and find something to feel positive about. He can think about his experiences and say, "Hey, look at what I accomplished…there's no way that I'm gonna let this problem beat me now." Whether he's facing a job interview, a test, or problems at home, the youth needs to be able to feel a sense of worth and self-esteem. The lessons he learned from Mother Nature and CCA will have helped prepare him for the many challenges he may face on his road through life.

CCA is a program designed to help kids learn academic and social skills and to accomplish tasks. As we develop the curriculum, we look at what we want to accomplish and then try to determine how we can present our findings to the kids in a structured manner. We know we need a plan to ensure that the kids acquire the skills and accomplish the tasks we present to them. We constantly strive for program lessons that keep the students engaged.

Although the list of our educational goals is short, it is very specific. We work toward ensuring that our program does the following:

- Allows interaction between students, teachers, and community members outside the classroom
- Integrates adaptive science, math, social studies and English into the students' learning
- Develops character and self-esteem through student-centered learning
- Builds bridges between cultures, ages, and socioeconomic statuses
- Demonstrates conservation practices and environmental respect
- Promotes a positive connection with the community
- Offers community job links and student references
- Takes a proactive approach toward firearm safety and education

This core agenda is our starting point—a place to focus our attention and a plan for building a structure that will be both engaging and challenging.

The physical space we call "Academy" is where the academic "book magic" happens, but even when the Academy is empty, we are still working with youth or searching for educational topics to help us all function better.

We use hunting, shooting, fishing, and conservation messages as the foundation for our year-round efforts, so it made sense for us to plan our curriculum around the traditional seasons for those activities. By using the different sporting seasons as the basis for our curriculum design, we are able to incorporate lessons that address real life seasonal situations while teaching something about the sporting opportunities that parallel those situations. By way of example, the early goose season is in September in Pennsylvania—just when the new school year starts. We created a *goose curriculum* to cover things like what guns are used to hunt geese, the types of licenses that are required (resident vs. non-resident) what recipes could be used for goose, and even how a goose compares to an airplane. We balance those lessons with discussions about what is happening at school—we may talk about something as basic as getting into their lockers and what their new schedules are like or more complex issues like whether or not they feel comfortable in their new school and their fears about the classes they are taking. At times, we use a goose call to enhance those conversations or to signal when students should do something specific.

We use what Mother Nature and society gives us to develop a year-round structure for learning. Let's go back to the goose hunting coursework. If a youth receives that lesson in his or her first year with the program and enjoys it, chances are he or she will return for a second year and go through that lesson again, but with modified supports to further enrich the learning. We knew that during the off-hunting seasons we could offer classes on other outdoor activities like ice fishing, but if the weather was nasty or it was too cold for the kids, we needed viable alternatives. It made perfect sense for us to use that time to work in some lessons around sports trade shows, the anatomy of firearms, and safety. For example, these lessons help keep the students current with what is happening in the sporting industry; they allow them to see what is new and exciting for the coming year; they provide refresher time to review safety concepts through role-play and discussion; and they give us the perfect forum for introducing CCA to the community if we decide to take a hands-on trip to a local indoor function.

When we are building our curriculum for a give program year, we rely heavily on the natural calendar. We look at what's happening in our area throughout the year. We look to see if there are any gun clubs offering youth field days or contests. If so, we tentatively plug that date in our calendar. We continually ask ourselves what can we do to develop our kids' knowledge base, and as our research evolves, our calendar starts to get very full. We take ideas from Mother Nature, from the seasons, from what's taking place in our community, from who's willing to help during the off season, etc.; and before we know it the key topics or events rise to the top and we have our curriculum for the coming year. One word of caution, just because you have an interest in a particular subject, that doesn't necessarily mean the kids will find it interesting. Take your interest and find its appeal, and then ask a few others for their input. If they think it can work, then give it a try. Worst case scenario is that you won't use that topic again next year. Each of our student academy meetings follows a specific format. This helps give the kids some structure and a set of expectations for each session. Here's how a typical weekly meeting breaks down when students come to us after school on Mondays:

Staff Expectations:

- Greet the participants and make kids feel welcome
- Conduct one-on-one dialogues about a self-reflection question
- Provide feedback for the students
- Oversee the students as refreshments are served and coach them on good table manners

- Review report cards and/or progress reports (6 week cycles)
- Help students with their homework if needed
- Give feedback about successes
- Address immediate needs and time related issues

Student Expectations:

- Arrive in their Academy uniform unless coming from work, in which case a work uniform is acceptable
- Adhere to all of the program rules
- Sign in when they arrive and get an attendance number
- Prepare to share their responses to the assigned self-reflection question, either in writing or verbally depending on their age
- Memorize a scope quote or a positive message
- Work on their personal folders and add their self-reflection information
- Complete a math warm-up if they have no homework
- Complete their shooting simulation activity

As a group, they may also:
- Share their self-reflection question responses
- Participate in group activities such as shooting, math skills, and riflery
- Share personal stories
- Discuss current events
- Complete a comprehensive academic lesson or art project
- Listen to a guest speaker
- Discuss the scope quote or positive message they memorized earlier and talk about its meaning

They'll end the session by
- Cleaning up the meeting space and reorganizing the materials
- Listening to announcements
- Participating in a raffle (periodically, when prizes are donated)

If there is an outdoor event or reward pending, Educational Staff may also
- Distribute and/or collect permission slips
- Provide crisis contact numbers and conduct email maintenance (Individuals)
- Conduct, support, and provide feedback for Conservation Education Field Trips
- Conduct, support, and share successes about shooting education classes (knowledge/skills with shotguns & rifles)
- Review formal written field trip reports and conduct 1-on-1 meetings to edit them
- Conduct study sessions in preparation for the Pennsylvania State Hunter Certification Test
- Work on Individual Conservation Education Plans (ICEPs) - 1-on-1
- Acquire, develop and organize hunting and fishing trip equipment and clothing
- Conduct hands-on travel activities and rewards (May include out-of-state travel)
- Introduce the guest speaker (Public Speaking) and/or offer feedback from field trips
- Award professional taxidermy services in recognition of individual hunting successes

- Offer college and job coaching and follow-up
- Create job references
- Discuss community service
- Participate in trade shows and fundraisers
- Work on senior projects with CCA—graded by the student's formal school
- Conduct ongoing private communications to discuss student goals, challenges, successes, etc.
- Participate in dinners, meetings and other events to learn community business networking
- Share our "Open Door" policy: our staff are available via 1 on 1 meetings, email, and/or by telephone

Field Reports

We have had numerous students publish field reports. A field report is a student's writings about his or her program experiences away from the Academy. It is not edited but rather is a free-write assignment. Only when a student decides that she or he personally wants to make the report better for publishing or to use at his or her formal school will we collaborate with them on the document. Their reports are kept in their work folders as concrete memories of the reward. We want to encourage a love of writing, and we believe that harsh criticism for a free write is not appropriate. A paper turned in about a joyous occasion that is returned covered with corrections that were not sought out can easily discourage a beginning writer. So with that in mind we encourage our students to follow a few guidelines. These guidelines will shape their writings but won't confine them. A trend we have seen is that as the students go on more trips they become more familiar with the process and their writings begin to open up and develop. That's the key: having them draw from within and then just write freely about their joy and fears—the known and the unknown. We also want them to write about what they saw, what they did, what they ate and how they lived. These writings can serve as a supplement at their formal schools, as a written trip diary, or as a pleasant read for the adults who experienced the trip with the youth.

There is probably nothing more exciting for CCA participants than to have his/her Field Report published. The academic and social benefits are extremely high. Nia's story appears in Universal Hunter Magazine (U.H.M.), which is CCA writing Partner.

Typically, our kids start with us in the 6th grade, just as they are entering the turbulent, challenging world of adolescence. These are years of great impact, ones in which many youth go astray. To combat that, youth need to feel confident of their self-worth and positive about their ability to succeed. That's where we come in—we help them along that road. We use hunting and shooting to accomplish this. Your passion may cause you to choose a different path of rewards. It doesn't matter what road you follow as long as you're committed to helping youth over a period of time beyond one day.

We look at the whole youth and ask, "How can we take strengths and weaknesses and work with the youth so that the weaknesses are addressed and the strengths become even more consistent?" And how can we take the families that have preconceived notions about the outdoors and firearms and detox them? We want our kids to become stronger. We want to know where they come from, what they like to do, what their backgrounds are, and what they like to listen to. We want to get in tune with the total youth, and to do this we have to connect and listen to that youth week after week.

When we take kids on a hunt reward trip, there is much more to it than just the actual hunting and shooting. We set many goals for that outing from getting up on time, to making sure they have their ammunition and the appropriate clothing, to practicing all the safety rules they have learned. They will already have learned a lot in the classroom about the animal we are hunting, say a turkey, but they will learn much more on the trip. If we are lucky enough to harvest a turkey, they'll know immediately that it's been a successful hunt, but even if we don't get a turkey on that trip, we want them to know that it was still a great experience. We want them to understand that they succeed either way because of all that they have learned that will be used to foster their success in the real world. A reward trip is a multi-faceted mission, and nothing teaches life lessons better than when we compete against Mother Nature. If the kids have the honor of shooting an animal, it will make them proud. If they don't get that honor, the adults need to help them feel proud about what it took for them to get there.

Prepared and dressed for "game day"—Let's go!

We teach our students that Mother Nature guarantees nothing more than the opportunity to experience its magnificence. She doesn't care about the numbers of people involved, what you look like, or where you live. She's willing to let you in if you appropriately embrace her.

1 out of 4, or 4 out of 4, we compete hard in outdoor sports—and simultaneously learn a lot about life.

The whole point is to help kids navigate through their complex world while learning multiple important lessons that will help them succeed in life. If they succeed, society succeeds. Our goal is not only to develop good hunters and shooters but also to develop good academic kids, good social kids and good adult citizens. My passion is hunting and shooting because that is what helped me when I was a kid growing up in difficult circumstances. I now use hunting and shooting as the vehicles to teach others the lessons I learned and of course to instill a love for our hunting heritage and a respect for nature. Your passion may be something entirely different, but whatever you choose—basketball, chess, cooking—you can use those values to teach life lessons and develop successful kids.

CHAPTER SIX:
Program Expectations, Evaluations and Awards

We set the bar high for our students at CCA. We give them their expectations right up front so they know what they're getting into and make it clear what the consequences are if they don't adhere to the rules. We are dealing with youth, and we need to make sure that they, and their parents or guardians, know that they will be safe and engaged while they're with us if they follow the rules.

We have set up a fairly comprehensive student code of conduct that is available to students when they join CCA. I'll briefly touch on some of these expectations here. Most are consistent with issues our students face every day—at home, in school, or in the community at large.

CCA is open to students of both genders (surprisingly, about 60 percent of our students are female) and of any race or national/ethnic origin. As such, we expect our students to demonstrate respect for one another.

Attendance – We know that absences interrupt learning for the student who is away, but they are also distracting for the instructors and other students. Of course, we recognize that there are some circumstances that make attending class impossible. We work with students to make up missed assignments in those instances, but otherwise, students need to recognize that membership is a commitment and attend classes regularly. We do subscribe to the philosophy

"If you miss CCA, you miss out."

Effort – Our students are expected to make a conscientious effort to finish their classroom work completely and on time. The class work lays the foundation for the more practical application of skills.

Following the Rules – Without rules and regulations, it would be easy for things to fall into chaos. We set our rules to make sure the students feel safe and their parents or guardians feel confident about what takes place at CCA and on our excursions.

Care for the facilities – We expect our students to help us keep our campus safe and well cared for. Everyone is responsible for taking care of all equipment and materials made available to them and for making sure our space is clean and organized before they leave at the end of a session.

Respect – Our students must demonstrate respect for our staff, the other students, and anyone else involved in the educational process. Our students represent CCA and are our face to the community; we want them to be our ambassadors regardless of where they are.

Dress Code – An extension of respect is self-respect. We have a dress standard for our kids that ensure they always look well groomed. This is why one of our first expectations is for students to wear their CCA shirts. A sense of sameness and belonging is extremely important to today's youth…just ask the Bloods, Crips, and Latin Kings.

CHAPTER SIX 93

Being unified in dress when traveling reinforces CCA participants (who might otherwise be uncomfortable in a new place) feeling they are part of a group. It also fosters them feeling the trip is special. Further, uniform dress underscores how organized our program is, and how business-like it is when appropriate. What do you think?

Obey the Law – While it seems overkill to state this as a rule, we want our kids to know that we expect them to obey the law at all times, both in the field and on the street.

Language – With so much exposure to obscene language on the radio, on TV, in books…virtually everywhere…many kids don't even realize there is anything wrong with it. We expect our staff to set an example for our kids by refraining from using off-color words or phrases, and prohibit such language from anyone using CCA facilities or while on excursions.

Internet Access and Use – While we recognize the value of having easy access to information when students are doing research for classes, we also know how easy it is for them to get onto inappropriate sites or for predators to take advantage of them via social networks. To keep our kids safe, we set very stringent rules around the internet and systems access while they are with us.

Bullying and Cyber Bullying – Bullying has been around forever, but Cyber Bullying is a relatively new demon for our kids to face. It came into its own with the easy access and anonymity of the internet. We want our students to have an environment that is free of bullying so they can concentrate on learning. We take a strong stand when we discover bullying among our students and strongly encourage students to report bullying when they see it or experience it—whether at home, in school, or anywhere else.

Note: You can visit oneface.me to see the Regional Emmy nominated video featuring our CCA students regarding Cyber Bullying.

Gangs – We can't stress enough that we want a safe environment for our kids, and gangs threaten the very heart of what we're striving to accomplish. We consider a gang three or more individuals with a common interest, bond, or activity whose purpose includes the commission of illegal acts or hate crimes and who refer to themselves by a group name or designation. Students may not wear or display anything that indicates they are members of a gang or that they have any gang affiliations. They may not use any gang specific language or gesture that associates them with gangs. On the upside of wearing colors, our color is orange. We wear that color proudly.

Harassment – We have established and pledge to maintain an educational environment totally free from sexual harassment.

Drugs – We prohibit and won't tolerate the unauthorized possession, use, distribution and/or sale of any illegal substances.

Tobacco – We recognize the hazards inherent to the use of tobacco products and the potential harm they pose for both smokers and nonsmokers; therefore, we don't allow the use or possession of any tobacco products.

A. Evaluations

We found that the simplest way to evaluate students was to use the process we use in school. Students move from one year to the next in concert with the school calendar and based on how much time they spend with us. The kids relate to this method because "it's what they're doing in school already." As they move up in school, they also move through the levels of our program.

Most of our students start with us in the 6th grade, but based on the student's age and specific needs, it may make more sense to aggressively move a student from the exploration level to extension, and then shorten the extension level to get them to the application level more quickly.

We also evaluate students in a manner similar to the way a football or softball team might. We look at the students' attitudes, determine what they are willing to give and how hard they are willing to work, and what steps they have taken to show that they're committed to the program. A really good evaluation may offer a student the opportunity to move from one phase or level to the next sooner.

Our first-level students begin to work hard and move through the Exposure and Exploration levels in their first year with the program. They must take the Hunter Safety Course and test before they can move on to the Application level. The Hunter Safety Test is a state certified test that shows the student's true commitment to the program. If a student decides not to take the Hunter Safety Test, it may be because they aren't totally committed to applying all of the skills they are learning at CCA. The Hunter Safety Test is a requirement before students can go any further in the program. We encourage them to take the test even if they choose not to hunt because we want them to feel good about passing a state test. The Hunter Safety Test is our concrete way to transition students from the lower levels in the program into the Application phase.

Once students get their orange hunter safety card, they don't ever have to take the test again, and even when they're adults if they choose to hunt, they'll be able to move forward with opportunities. We find that taking the hunter safety test is a big positive for our kids and their families. There are written evaluations that are sometimes given, and depending on what the circumstances are, you may want to evaluate a trip and decide who's qualified based on a current student's functioning for upcoming rewards.

B. Rewards

Yes, we have a plethora of awards that we give to youth throughout the levels. Getting a uniform to belong to CCA—which is their t-shirt—is the first opportunity to be recognized that you are good enough and you're showing society that you want to become better—that you're willing to work in a program and work towards goals. The second reward our kids get is to travel to various places for dinners. We're really big believers in eating with our youth because the bond that you gain over mealtime is irreplaceable and priceless. It would be in an organizations' best interest to invite the kids more frequently to the dinners they hold to promote their agendas. They're a prime opportunity to start relationships that can bring new life into a mostly elder represented organization. (A rewards list is in the Appendix.)

Snack time at the Academy includes teaching good manners.

Applying CCA taught manners and other social skills at events are fun. Here some of our participants are at one of the banquets put on by local conservation organizations like the Lehigh Valley Chapter of Safari Club International. Such a "night out" is one of the fun rewards our kids can earn based on their CCA performance.

Beyond the opportunities to eat, students may also get to experience a store—Cabela's for instance—for a more traditional field trip. These are lower-level rewards for kids that are still exploring or extending. Once they get to the Effective Application stage, they're eligible for every type of hunting and fishing trip you can imagine. The sky's the limit based on what and with whom we can connect. These rewards can range anywhere from a squirrel hunt, to a sporting clay shoot, to a deer hunt, to a boar hunt, to getting on a plane to hunt geese or ducks in another state, or to flying to Canada. Don't think small when you think about your rewards (do think it through though—it doesn't really make sense to spend thousands of dollars to fly kids to hunt doe when you might be able to hunt doe in your own state for one-fifth the cost). Costs will usually dictate the reward decision.

To our way of thinking, the bigger the reward, the more work the kid has done. This philosophy aligns with the continuity of the program. You don't give a trip to Canada to a kid you don't know yet. I see a lot of that in the current industry, a name is drawn out of a hat and a kid is taken hunting. I look at that and think they don't know anything about the kid's growth. That's not to say that the kid isn't getting something from the event, but in our program, our system, we want to make sure that that special opportunities are maximized. We want to be sure the youth have worked for a reward, and that, in turn, they have internalized it and will take more ownership over it. That way, they tend to be more respectful, and to embrace and to love that adventure so much more. The recognition and rewards will come as the kids grow in your program.

One of the ultimate rewards for our kids is taxidermy. In a lot of programs they stop their efforts a little early. We want to give our kids classroom shooting instruction and to expose them to live shooting and instruction, and then we want them to apply it in a competition with Mother Nature and then give them their trophy. When we say a trophy, it's personal and size does not matter. They can take a piece of taxidermy back to their homes and share it with other people in their community. I think that some of the best advice we can offer people is to go the extra step and get some taxidermy done and then present it in a public forum to celebrate the youth. Keep in mind, taxidermy turn-around is slow (it usually averages about a year), so make sure to get some photos taken to hold your young hunter over until the day of celebration. That youth will hang onto you for a year to get their mount—that's a classic example of extension. When a youth takes a deer head to his or her home, and shares it with the 15 or 18 people that might enter that home during that year, the ripple effect becomes pretty great, especially when he or she lives in a non-hunting environment. We look at our taxidermy as our largest reward—our largest concrete reward for having our youth say, "I have accomplished this task." You can give certificates out, and yes, they do have some meaning (a hunter safety certificate is a great way to recognize a kid for his work), but we try to give our kids their taxidermy in a celebratory event. It's the best advertising the hunting and shooting industry could ask for. Taxidermists are overlooked and under-appreciated. We're very lucky to have the Pennsylvania Taxidermy Association supporting us. They have done more for the image of hunting than many other sporting organizations that are purely hunting focused. I don't even think the Pennsylvania Taxidermy Association recognizes how vital they are to the continuity of our kid's story about what they have accomplished. As a side note: If you can't get taxidermy done for an award or reward, then you definitely want to be sure you're using photos—BIG, BEAUTIFUL photos. I cannot stress enough how the kids value the opportunity to use pictures to support their stories. The smiles on their faces are definitely a reward; it's a reward for your supporters, a reward for your volunteers, a reward to the people who have given their time and who want to believe they've made a difference in kids' lives. The biggest extrinsic rewards in our program are taxidermy and photographs. You can also use text messages, emails, and phone calls—all of those things help kids build self-esteem. A phone call two days after seeing a kid do something and reinforcing what he or she has accomplished can be a very strong award, so look at the rainbow of all that you can offer a youth. But just remember, the pot of gold—for getting into virgin advertising space—is taxidermy and in-hand photos.

Taxidermy is a vital resource for CCA participant recruitment and retention. Annually, the Pennsylvania Taxidermy Association celebrates our students' successes. They have helped us for more than 15 years. Together we have put more youth mounts in "unreachable places" like inner city living rooms than anyone in the world.

Individualized Conservation Education Plan (ICEP)

We use a process at our academy called an ICEP (Individualized Conservation Education Plan). We use our ICEP after we have determined the participant is committed to our program. It's a tool we can use to try to get an idea as to where the youth is and where that youth might want to go. It's a working document used over a long period of time—we have kids that have worked on this document for 4, 5, and 6 years. They write down their goals, what they would like to learn, what they'd like to see, and what they'd like to accomplish. We usually start this in the Extension stage, and that becomes an official working document while with us. It's a great framework for students that are going into the higher levels of the program and formal school. It provides some good, solid information about the youth; you gain some solid documentation of growth that you can show to the kids to help them see how they, including their ideas, have changed over time. You can also use it when kids are impulsive and want to do or have something now. Going over the ICEP with them can show them how their ideas and feelings have changed as they have grown and developed. For example, a youth may first think he or she wants to be a veterinarian, and then over time he realizes that what he really wants is to be a surgeon. We can tell that individual wants to help something or someone, so we encourage that student to search out jobs related to his interests and have him determine the minimum schooling and steps he will have to pursue to get there.

☑ Tips/Reminders

- ☑ A successful way to incorporate "multi-mission mentoring" into your program is to start with short- term and immediate goals. You might set up goals over the next three weeks. They might be as simple as seeing that the dishes are done, being on time, or completing all homework assignments. Then look at those goals and determine how we can help affect them in a positive manner. The philosophy behind this is to allow the youth to be structured by the little missions put in front of them. Collaborate on little goals and then combine them to accomplish the mission of building the total youth.
- ☑ By giving our kids multiple missions, we allow for successes, mistakes and failures in a safe environment. The structure we provide assures us that there will be learning, growth, and success. We keep presenting our kids with small missions throughout their time with us. These goals revolve around school, home, and community. Mentoring our youth through these incremental steps helps them attain success.

Think about Lego's. You stack one on top of another and before you know it they are transformed into a solid structure.

"Girls don't hunt! Especially inner-city, minority girls," a passerby quipped. Well, yes, they do hunt—and with passion! It's personally rewarding for them and us to be part of something that isn't supposed to happen. CCA loves the frequency with which we have "beat the odds" regarding urban youth successfully participating in outdoor sports.

CHAPTER SEVEN:
Participant Recruitment, Samples of Tools Used, and Equipment and Storage

A. Recruiting and Selecting CCA Participants

In the beginning, I just offered my program to students in my classes at the school where I teach. Over time, word spread—through the kids, their parents or guardians, sponsors, and my participation in trade shows and community events—and soon others begin asking about the program. Because we had limited resources with regard to meeting space and available volunteers, we developed a selection process for admittance.

Youth have to demonstrate a real interest in the program to get into its Extension and Application phases; if they do make it, we assess their schoolwork and review their report cards to discover their strengths and opportunities for improvement. We meet with them individually to lay out our expectations for them, and we observe them in group settings to get a sense of the whole youth. We tell them right up front that this will be a lot of work. We also talk to their families to be sure that there is permission for the youth's participation. The Exploration phase is when some kids decide the program isn't right for them, some are eliminated due to conflicts, and some just didn't quite meet our expectations. We may feel they don't have a strong desire to take on the commitment, they may be over-extended already, they may not have the fortitude or maybe they just can't get parental consent. Regardless of the reason, being told they didn't make the cut will always come with a "please find something you enjoy doing and definitely continue to try new things."

We really hate to disappoint kids, and when they want to join CCA but aren't selected, we meet with them and go over the reason(s) why. Many times these meetings give them some specific things to focus on so they can successfully reapply at a later time. You could think of CCA as being like a baseball farm system. Not being selected doesn't mean they won't ever get to join us for an event. When we have large exploration events, we try to include everyone we can. Sometimes attending a second event sparks a strong desire in the student, and he or she goes crazy trying to get deeper into the program. That's actually a great problem for us to have.

Regardless of the fact that they weren't selected, we're still trying to build relationships with them, but it's hard to build relationships even as you're trying to sever them. That's not to say we don't occasionally make mistakes. We find ourselves wondering why kids that barely made it through the selection process are still with us 3 or 4 years later, or why kids that were so gung-ho when they started burned out after 2 or 3 months. It's something that we need to look at scientifically and determine what we could do better to make us even stronger.

Getting past the Exploration phase of the program is and into the Extension level of the system is a selective and time-dictated process. That's one of the reasons why we maintain a wait list for the academy. If a seat becomes available (through attrition due to a move or loss of interest, etc.) we can move another youth right into the opening. There is, of course, a lesson that comes with not being selected or in a choice not to continue, and that lesson is reality.

The bottom line is that we're looking for kids that are in it for the long haul—"lifers." We know that some will try it for a little while and decide that it just isn't for them, but we try to minimize our dropout rate by conducting a diligent survey of our applicant's qualities. Selecting the right kids, from the onset, is not based upon the honor roll nor being in the juvenile justice system. I would guess that eighty-five percent of the youth that make it into our upper levels are just normal kids with the normal aspirations of all teens, and with our support they can become young adults that have reached their untapped potential.

> "There's a difference between interest and commitment. When you're interested in doing something, you do it only when circumstances permit. When you're committed to something, you accept no excuses, only results."
>
> ### Jim Ike Eichinger

When you help a boy grow into a young man and he gives your efforts to help him "props and luv," how rewarding is that? Pictured above is David as a 6th grader (insert) and as a man serving our country. He uses Facebook to keep in contact with us. Many of our successful graduates still check-in via social media to let us know they how they are doing.

B. Samples of Tools Used

Effective implementation of CCA requires credible/useful tools to be employed. In addition to the before described Individualized Conservation Education Plan (ICEP), two other samples of tools we use are these: Annual Program Calendar of Events; and Field Reports and How to Write Them. A copy of each is provided in the book's Appendices.

C. Equipment and Storage

When I first started this program, I relied on my own equipment or borrowed it from friends, but as the program grew, I knew I'd need more equipment than I could supply. There are many cost-efficient ways to accumulate materials. Here are just a few of the ways we equip our kids. We ran community equipment drives for used tents and fishing rods—these events usually brought in more gear than we needed. At trade shows, we rented booths and posted lists of the items we were looking for to move our program forward. We found that people stopping by our booth were happy to support us. We sent that same list out to rod and gun clubs, and also posted it on Facebook with great success.

As always, it comes down to relationships. If you can befriend someone connected with a local gun shop, he may be a good resource when you need help. Let him know what you are looking for, chances are he'll share the information with his patrons. People are always trading in their guns, and your organization may benefit from someone's generosity.

One important note here the whole issue of acquiring

various guns for our youth is complicated. It is critically important that you match the appropriate gun to the right youth. Getting the correct gauge and caliber for the weight and age of the youth will mean the difference between a bad first shooting experience and a positive one.

There is a lot of other equipment necessary for successful outings. It's our responsibility to be sure the kids have the correct boots and clothing for the area they'll be visiting. For us, that means we need the right resources and we need to be organized and do complete advance planning. We make lists and checklists, leaving nothing until the last minute and certainly leaving nothing to chance.

Getting equipment is only half the battle. Now that you have it, where do you store it? In the beginning, you will undoubtedly have to store everything at your own home, but as your tools and equipment grow, you may need a larger storage space. We had to find more space fairly early on. This is another place that you can rely on your resources and contacts to help you make the necessary arrangements. One thing to add: make sure you have unlimited access to your gear and firearms. No one wants to be called at the very last minute, especially if it's 3 a.m.

CHAPTER EIGHT:
Formal Evaluation of CCA's Effectiveness/Success

(Some information in this section is principally extracted from a 2014 document: *CCA Comprehensive Evaluation System.* **So hold on tight!**)

A. Feedback and Awards

CCA has always collected useful evaluative data. The diverse evaluation methods used to do so have included requiring written/typed reports from participants regarding CCA field trips in which they were involved, accepting unsolicited thank-you notes/cards from participants and their parents or guardians, collecting unsolicited CCA write-ups and special features from varied print and television media, and occasionally distributing and collecting formal surveys of participants and/or their parents or guardians. Over the years, data from such evaluative methods have suggested CCA's principal success indicators include the following:

- Participants' high attendance rate;
- Participants' impressive degree of involvement in program activities;
- High percentage of participants who remain in the CCA for more than one year;

- Applicant demand for acceptance into CCA chronically exceeding available resources/capacity;
- The types, number and content of the unsolicited letters, notes, calls and emails from participants and their family members;
- Rate at which participants pass the Pennsylvania state hunters' education exam;
- Number of very positive write-ups and special features about CCA in varied print and television media outlets, such as the NBC Nightly News, CNN, America's First Freedom, Universal Hunter Magazine, and the book *The Future of the Gun.* Such sources have lauded CCA for the following: leadership quality, unique program components, participant demographics, and high degree of overall success; and, contribution to the community; and,
- Formal surveys of participants and their parents or guardians citing increases in participants' confidence and self-esteem, useful academic and social knowledge and skills, and being likely to become a good community member. These results align with these key adolescent development areas: self-concept/perception, cognitive/academic, social and emotional.

Further, CCA has earned external recognition via awards such as the Pope and Young Stewardship Award and A McDonald's Excellence in Education Award for its delivery of innovative lessons and caring components.

As CCA's CEO and Founder, I have also received awards for my work with youth.

The Liberty Bell Award had always been presented to lawyers and judges...until my work with youth came along. Also, being named to the Outdoor Life 25 was very exciting and rewarding!

B. Comprehensive Evaluation System

Obviously, the CCA evaluation results and awards are appreciated and valuable, and will continue to be so. But until recently CCA, like many important programs for our underprivileged youth, focused itself so much on fostering adolescent development basics—including simultaneously assisting our participants in dealing with associated life exigencies. Therefore, CCA has had comparatively limited financial resources, and associated professional time and expertise, available to periodically design and conduct more comprehensive and scientifically systemic evaluations of the CCA's effectiveness (e.g., a longitudinal study). So to address this, CCA has established a relationship with Ridley & Associates (R&A), LLC, a human and organization development entity (in Washington DC) to assist in developing and implementing our *Comprehensive Evaluation System*. R&A's expertise includes developing and evaluating test/assessment instruments, and designing and implementing research and surveys, and evaluation and performance facilitation/management systems. Further, R&A's CEO and President is an adolescent development expert.

R&A has completed a review of all of CCA's governance documents, the content of its varied forms of evaluative feedback—including previous surveys, and visited our physical location on multiple occasions to gain *first-hand* experience regarding how the CCA program actually operates. CCA and R&A agreed that the Comprehensive Evaluation System will be clearly aligned with the long-standing quality and integrity of CCA's program. To help facilitate that, CCA has readily agreed to adopt and increasingly use R&A's CARE

3-StepTM model for enhancing personnel and organizational performance.

Data from our CCA's new evaluation system has began to reinforce the importance of CCA continuing to do what it has done successfully for many years. Such data has also began being used to refine and expand components of CCA's multi-faceted program, and to provide our actual/prospective stakeholders the information needed to better decide if and how they should be involved in CCA in meaningful and mutually beneficial ways. Accordingly (and consistent with the CARE 3-StepTM model), CCA will produce annual and/or as-needed surveys of participants, their parents or guardians, program staff, and other prospective/actual supporting shareholders (e.g., *in-kind*, financial, equipment, and supplies). Further, the resultant evaluative data also will be provided to shareholder groups and entities—as appropriate. Moreover, the enhanced comprehensiveness and scientific quality of our evaluation data can better enable us to aid others in deciding if they would like to replicate and/or extend the CCA in other geographic locations, especially in the United States.

C. Computerized Database

CCA started using a computer database in 2011 to help keep track of basic information about its program, especially its participants. Previously, that had been done just with hand-written documents. During the previous CCA program year, that database's structure and content started being refined/expanded to better accommodate acquiring, maintaining and using the types of information needed for the CCA evaluation system's future statistical analyses and reports. The preceding will also be aided by refining/expanding the standardized (and *psychometrically-sound*) forms and test/assessment instruments CCA uses to collect data placed into the database. CCA and R&A is ensuring that such data are housed in at least two locations for safety and avoiding loss.

D. Comprehensive Evaluation System Reports

CCA has begun constructing and maintaining an ongoing series of three types of evaluation synopsis/summary reports. *Brief Evaluation Report (BER), Shareholder Evaluation Report* (SER) and *Prospective Shareholder Evaluation Report* (PSER). Each report type has a standardized format that can be appropriately customized for a specific shareholder audience.

I realize the last chapter might have been a lot to take in. We aren't playing around when it comes to our efforts for children. Now onto some easier-to-process information for the remainder of the book.

CHAPTER NINE: Financial Support for Youth Programs

I was at a trade show trying to find support for my program when a "youth investing" business partner of a friend told me to "stop walking around with your hand out." He had made a ton of money selling items that targeted youth and I made the ASSUMPTION (yes, I know all about the 'A** out of U and Me' saying!) that he might be interested in going a little deeper than his current investment in products. He had the unmitigated nerve to tell me I was out of line for asking for help. Frankly, I wanted to hammer him because my hand wasn't out for me; it was out for my kids and our mission of promoting the outdoors. Asking for support was what I needed to do to keep my program running and help as many kids as I possibly could. Of course, I didn't say anything rude to him, but to this day I get angry when I think about that incident. Here was a man who had made a lot of money from his products, yet he begrudged me asking for a small contribution (and I mean small) for a cause in the same niche where he made all of his money. His decision to not support was exactly that, his decision. He was entitled to give where he saw fit. I learned a lot from that incident. It was my first indication that smoke and mirrors existed in the industry. What I mean is, the hunting and shooting outdoor industry always told me in their messaging to take a kid hunting, and I was doing just that, but I couldn't get help to implement that message. It was a tough life lesson. Time and time again I heard "Kids,

Kids, Kids," and yet I didn't really feel the voices were sincere. I had to move on—and I did. I am still amazed at a lot of the conversations I hear regarding the youth in the hunting and shooting sports. I've never been much of a talker—more of a doer—but it seems to me that if the hunting and shooting sports are going to survive, the doers better start showing up because talking without action is wasted air.

It's a fact of life that you can't run a program without funds. When I first began to put my vision, my dream, my passions, into action, I did so with very little money, and most of what I spent was my own. A critical question to ask yourself is, "What can I commit; how much can I afford to give?" I knew that I was willing to give back as much as I could to help kids succeed and to what "saved me." It takes resources to take what I refer to as "NOCs" (Nontraditional Outdoor Youth) on overnight hunting trips—especially on those trips where multi-night travel and licensing costs could add up.

A lot more doors (and hopefully pockets) will open for you if you are a nonprofit because the certification not only documents your "government legitimacy," but it also allows donors to write off some of what they give you. You *will* still have to raise funds, and you can only do that by proving your own personal worth and the value of your program. Your credibility and professional reputation are your most valuable assets. People have to understand your mission, see your love, and believe in what you are doing. More importantly, *you* have to believe in what you're doing. Don't bother to go after funds if you don't believe in yourself and your true meaning; it just won't work. Oh, I'm sorry, it can work if you have a crafty marketing effort, but you will eventually be labeled a paper champion and that won't get the job done.

Fundraising isn't easy; yes, money is available, but lots of people are after the same dollars you're seeking. You have to get out and show people your vision and your passion and ask, ask, ask. Don't be shy. If you feel uncomfortable asking for money start practicing, and just remember your desire to help kids should trump any reservations you might have. (To this day I'm still practicing!) Do whatever you can to develop relationships and get your message out. You have to be seen. The more you can develop true and sincere relationships with people, the better your chances of getting support from them. You need to continually respect and stay true to your vision and current supporters even while you develop new relationships. Also try to stay on top of giving habits you discover. If you get turned down, do not give up. Go back and ask why you were turned down. Ask why they wouldn't choose to give to an organization like yours? Ask what you can to do to change their minds? What would they like to see? Caution: **DO NOT** change your values and your vision for the almighty dollar. If you are offered support and feel in your gut that it's going to compromise your mission, leave the money on the table. There have been many funding opportunities that we have turned down because they would have required us to push another agenda, and for me that was unacceptable. Keep plugging, light a fire under those people with whom you share your message, and let them see and feel your passion. It will eventually pay off. It may only be a happy meal-sized payoff, but there is always a prize in that box, so look for it. If you find this approach difficult, just remember whom this is for—our youth are at stake here.

I was told more than once that if I would switch our program from hunting and shooting to the safer fishing route I would be able to raise all the funds I'd ever need. I gave that suggestion a lot of thought; after all it was tempting to think I would be able to secure funds more easily. It is a fact that there are people and organizations totally opposed to shooting and hunting. We have been denied grants for that very reason. Committees and board members have that right to decide where their money goes. I knew what saved me as a young boy growing up in difficult circumstances. It was nature, animals, the woods and, yes, hunting and shooting. I knew I could only succeed with my dream of helping other young people if I stayed true to my core values. And so I respectfully said no and continued to decline the alternate routes suggested by those who wanted me to change the way we at CCA help America's youth.

You know, there's nothing like going fishing to beat the "non-hunting season blues."

CCA's fishing trip rewards are also appreciated by our participants. Compared to hunting/shooting trips, fishing trips take less training and the travel is often a lot easier. Further, fishing is less difficult to "sell" to society as an appropriate outdoor sport in which our youth should engage in.

A. 2 Million Bullets

Over the years, we have made many attempts to raise funds—some successful, and some a complete waste of time. We always knew there was a bigger picture we needed to see, and it took a divine moment after a tragic incident for it to appear. One of the saddest events in my life was when one of the students I was very close to was murdered. How I grieved for that young man. I kept thinking how much I wished I could be the bullet that took his life—then I could have redirected my path to an inanimate object towards something that didn't matter. That tragedy was the inspiration and provided momentum for the 2 Million Bullets Campaign. I thought that if we could find two million like-minded people willing to stand up for youth and give a dollar to become a Bullet, we could serve multitudes of young people across America with our proven programs. We could help them stay off the streets, avoid the influence of drugs and gangs, and develop into the productive young adults we knew they could be through outdoor education.

Through the pain of that loss, and with some guidance from above, we have developed a major fund raising and awareness campaign called 2 Million Bullets. The orange ribbon is the symbol of that campaign. A ribbon in society shows you care about something. The mission of 2MB serves a dual purpose: 1) Adults proudly wear our orange ribbons to create awareness. When people see them they often open a dialogue about the symbol. This gives us a great opportunity to explain our passion for caring for youth through the hunting and shooting culture. 2) We ask people to support our program by purchasing an orange ribbon for a dollar—they are welcome to donate more if they like. When you display or wear an orange ribbon, people will inevitably ask about it, and you can explain that the orange ribbons are the symbol of Two Million Bullets ("Two" and "2" are used interchangeably). They are a visible reminder that adults wearing them care about youth and are making them the focal point of the hunting and shooting heritage. For too many years, we've placed the importance of the critters in front of our youth. Think about it; there are organizations for every critter under the sun, yet after all these years, we still don't have a symbol to show the world that WE (hunters and gun owners) care about kids; that one unifying symbol that brings all of us together under one umbrella for our youth. Since no one else has done it—and believe me, I wish they had—we decided to do it ourselves to help America become buoyant in its declining public perception of hunters and shooters.

The country, especially mainstream America, needs to know that we don't just care about guns, shooting, the Second Amendment and hunting, but that we care about youth and the future of our great outdoor traditions. How are we doing that, currently? The right response is NOT EFFECTIVELY! How many youth commercials do you see on outdoor television? I encourage you to adopt an orange ribbon… put one on your hat, your suit, and on your truck. Prove to society that you have a human side as a gun owner or a hunter and that you do care about youth and what their future will be. I hope you will act now and become a Bullet.

Imagine what could be accomplished for the youth and the outdoor sports of hunting and shooting if those of you reading this book went out for 2, 3, or 4 weekends and promoted the message of the orange bullet ribbons, or even placed a large orange ribbon in your place of business. We could come together under one symbol with a united goal to help America's children become upstanding adults through America's hunting and shooting heritage. Major League Baseball and the National Football League have different teams playing under common symbols. It's time that we—a separatist industry of shot gunners, hand gunners, elk hunters, deer hunters, and all the other subgroups—unite under a common symbol for our youth. We might choose different paths in our lives, it doesn't matter; the orange ribbon could become the universal symbol for adults helping and proving they care about kids in the hunting and shooting industry. You can visit 2millionbullets.org to learn more.

My great hope is this: people will recognize that our youth should be at the top of the list for our good-hearted efforts. This awareness movement will do a lot to poke holes in society's stereotypes about the shooting and hunting culture and its perceived lack of caring. After all, it is our responsibility to provide our youth with a bridge that leads to our great outdoor traditions. *Two Million Bullets* has the power to be that bridge.

> I want to be the bridge to the next generation.
>
> **Michael Jordan**

Some Relevant Statistics

- Without charities and nonprofits, America would simply not be able to operate. According to a Giving USA 2013 report, total contributions in 2012 exceeded $316.23 billion dollars
- In 2012, there were more than 1.4 million organizations that formally obtained recognition for their tax-exempt status with the IRS
- Two studies from The Chronicle found that online gifts to America's nonprofits are growing far faster than other types of donations

The three snapshots above are on my desk at school where I teach. They are annual school pictures of the same student—Devon. He was killed in a senseless act of gun violence. His death prompted me to start 2millionbullets.org, the adult partner to CCA.

In the 2MB program, the word "bullet" refers to adults who hunt and/or shoot and care about youth. Bullets show society they care by wearing an orange ribbon which shows that they believe in giving youth a S.H.O.T. (i.e., Students Helped by Outdoor Traditions)

☑ Tips/Reminders

- ☑ Try to include some "money people" on your team—people who understand money and how to pitch your program.
- ☑ There is grant money available if you have the resources to pursue it. Applying for grants can be time consuming, but an experienced grant writer can be an enormously valuable asset.
- ☑ Make it possible for people to contribute to your organization on-line; this is the fastest growing avenue for donations.
- ☑ A typical truth about money: to get it, you have to ask for it.

The most organized and successful method we have found for seeking donations is to set up a calendar. Note all of the sources you want to approach. Go to each of them and find out what their "give away" schedule is. Find out what they need from applicants and let them know that you are going to ask for a donation. Talk to them about your success, how you can represent them, and why it would be in their best interest to align with you.

CHAPTER TEN:
Legal Issues

Liability, Insurance and Licensing

What do you mean I need insurance? When I first started CCA, I did not give any thought to the need for insurance. There were far more important things on my mind (like kids' lives). Eventually, however, as we grew, I began to think about the need for different type of insurance. I'm no expert and have only a few suggestions to offer. These are things I learned because of the path I had to walk to move CCA forward. Automobile issues are fairly common and easy to resolve because, as an individual volunteer, you can get special insurance riders that cover kids being transported in your car. You can visit nonprofitrisk.org for more details.

When I looked into liability insurance, I hit a wall, I couldn't get it. I went to every insurance company I could and was told there was no way I could be insured for letting inner-city or urban youth use firearms. This became a big issue because if others were promoting shooting and hunting as safe, we should have been able to get insurance. Eventually, I got a break when I talked with the National Rifle Association (NRA) and was able to get insurance through their club program.

If you are a 501(c)(3) organization, that deals with firearms, I advise you to consider reaching out to the NRA for insurance. They will be able to help you not only with your firearms-related insurance needs, but they can also help you with other types of insurance. If you're looking for insurance as an individual, get an insurance rider for your vehicle and insure yourself to the fullest extent possible. It doesn't cost that much money, and it will give you the peace of mind you need. It will also reassure parents or guardians knowing that you are insured and willing to go the extra mile to be "official."

When we are traveling to a specific place, we always check into the insurance provided. Most hunting venues, professional outfitters, guides, lodges, stores, etc., will carry insurance. Be sure you know what their insurance covers, and what yours covers. Knowing such facts and being able to present proof of insurance for both parties will make for more secure relationships.

There are insurance agents who deal primarily with insurance coverage for volunteer organizations. Aligning yourself with one of these agents can help immensely as you decide what insurance you need. Talk to your agent to gather any information he or she can offer until you feel comfortable enough to move forward.

It may take some time and effort to obtain an insurance policy, but it will be well worth it. After a few years of proving you are safe and responsible, you won't have any problem renewing your insurance. You can Google "insurance for nonprofit programs" or "volunteer insurance" to find a list of possibilities. I've talked about the licensing necessary to become certified as a nonprofit, 501(c)(3) organization. Although it is a time-consuming process, it is necessary if you hope to start your own federally recognized program. There is another option if the certification process is too overwhelming and costly for you. You might collaborate with a local conservation (or other) organization that is already certified. You may be able to put your vision in place as a sub-program under their 501(c)(3) status. Think it through; do you want your own entity, or do you want to support another entity with a youth focus? Explore the possibilities.

Fishing and hunting laws can vary from state to state. It is imperative that you become familiar with the laws of each state. It is easier now to get hunting licenses than it once was. In fact, you can get them online in some states, which is a big step up from waiting in line for hours like we did with our kids in the past. However, the actual license may still have to be mailed and that will add additional time, so confirm what the rules are and plan accordingly if you are going hunting soon. You may be able to print licenses that are acquired via the Internet and have them instantly. Just be sure to check in advance so that you know your options. We prefer that parents or guardians obtain their youth's hunting license because Pennsylvania requires a social security number. If that isn't possible, we ask the parents or guardians for the youth's social security number, birth date, and confirm the home address. We assure them once we get the license, we immediately destroy the social security number. The youth then is registered under his/her own social security number for the remainder of their lives and can acquire new licenses through the automated state system. Just because you know how to use an automated licensing service, do not assume it will be that easy for others. Be prepared to walk first timers through the steps and be patient. To many beginners, it's a foreign process of what tags, stamps and harvest reporting needs they will need to have to be in compliance.

Note: All of our youth are required to be state certified at the end of their first year. They put in two—sometimes three—years of class work until they reach the Application level at CCA where they actually go hunting.

Hunter safety certification is more than a test; it's a rite of passage for CCA students. Passing a state test for this certification has great meaning, especially in homes where parents or guardians may actually have a lingering fear of their own "educational past."

A student signs his hunting license, making it official. Nothing can ruin an experience like a fine or loss of recreational privileges. CCA participants know to sign their license as soon as they get it. The supervising adults know to remain aware of local game laws, especially those pertaining to youth; and, to take a picture of shooting times and keep it on their Smartphone along with licensing proof—just in case an immediate need arises.

CHAPTER ELEVEN:
Dealing with the Media

Getting support for your organization requires getting it noticed, and that means working with the press, local businesses, and entrepreneurs willing to back worthwhile projects. I have done a number of professional appearances in the name of outdoor sports such as hunting and shooting, and many weren't that friendly. It's easy to work with the media when friendly fire is protecting you. The challenge is when you go out on a limb and into the lion's den to get your point across. One of the very best things you can do for your organization is to build alliances within a number of communities so that others will speak on your behalf and open some doors. Also aligning your program with local colleges and universities can make it possible for you to leverage the physical and human resources they have to offer. This can prove to be a huge advantage when you are collecting data, writing articles or ads, and looking for web or messaging support.

Keep the lines of communication open. This can be done by getting articles and advertisements about your events, students, outings, and fund raising campaigns into the local papers, on the radio, and on the bulletin boards of local businesses. Make your print materials colorful and eye-catching. Use pictures whenever possible as people are naturally curious, and they would particularly like to see if they know anyone in the photo.

As you look at your team of volunteers, think about which of them might make a good publicist for your group—

someone with a "gift for gab," but who doesn't run on forever. Choose someone that can readily establish relationships with people who can share your news and promote your events—someone who is reliable. Sit down with such persons and draw up some goals for a communications plan. That will make it easier on everyone because the expectations will be clear.

Test your communications goals and plan by having trial runs with a group of people close to you. They can help you spot errors, weaknesses, and discrepancies in the message before you send it to the population at large. Having materials that are written clearly and free of errors will go a long way in establishing your credibility; and a solid communication delivered in a positive tone will help you sell your organization to potential students, parents or guardians, donors and the community.

One thing to keep in mind when working with the media is that there is always the potential for controversy to crop up. In our case, there are people who feel teaching youth to use firearms and to hunt is a travesty. By working with the media (instead of against it) we have been able to share with readers/listeners how educating youth about respect for firearms and how to safely use them may actually prevent tragic accidents. Just remember doubters aren't necessarily the enemy; they may have legitimate questions and concerns, and it's our job to put their minds at ease as much as possible. However, there are those who will use all of their energy to derail your train. Focusing on the word "education" can help you in your rebuttals.

CHAPTER ELEVEN 139

Sometimes, working with the media is easy because it aligns with your mission; but, you can end up in the "lion's den" where you "face the enemy." Be prepared for both, and use everyday conversations to train for these big events.

☑ Tips/Reminders

- ☑ Assign one or two members of your group to become well versed on all hunting and fishing laws. Have them available via phone or email should you need a second opinion. The last thing you want is to make a mistake in the field that could adversely impact the day, the kids, the mission, and the program.
- ☑ Befriend a game warden or commissioner to give you advice and offer shortcuts for getting the information you need on relevant issues.
- ☑ Carry shooting times on your smart phone.
- ☑ Don't forget to follow reporting or tagging procedures. It's easy to get so wrapped up in a celebration that you miss something.
- ☑ It's as simple as it sounds: double check that the license has been signed by the youth.
- ☑ Put together a poster or a handout list of items that members of the community might be able to donate.
- ☑ Document where items will be stored and how it will be used and by whom.
- ☑ Use this list when you build your activity calendar so you can plan effectively for the loaning and returning of materials.
- ☑ If borrowing materials or equipment be sure your plans take into consideration the amount of time it will take to get the gear and then return it after the outing. Don't forget clothing will need to be washed.

A final thought on CCA.

Whether in the field or at a dinner, if our "clients" are happy, then we're happy. Happiness through successful personal effort is what we strive to give to each CCA participant year after year.

APPENDICES

A. List of Sponsors, Partners and Donors
B. List of Rewards
C. Program's Annual Calendar of Events
D. Field Reports and How to Write Them
E. Personalized Help for You and/or Your Organization

A. List of Partners and Sponsors

Donors of money

- Anonymous and Announced Individual Donor(s) Across the Nation.

Sponsor Awards Via Grants

- Lehigh Valley Chapter of Safari Club International, Lehigh Valley Pennsylvania
- Lehigh Valley Chapter of Friends of NRA, Lehigh Valley Pennsylvania
- Campfire Conservation Fund, Chappaqua New York
- Lehigh County Community Foundation, Pennsylvania
- Leupold & Stevens Inc., Beaverton Oregon
- Allentown Rotary Club, Allentown Pennsylvania
- Sertoma Club of Allentown, Allentown Pennsylvania
- Eastern Chapter of the Foundation North American Wild Sheep, Brownstown Pennsylvania

- Larry the Cable Guy's Git 'R Done Foundation in conjunction with Cabela's, Eau Claire Wisconsin
- Pennsylvania Chapter of Rocky Mountain Elk Foundation, Montrose Pennsylvania
- Cornell University Lab of Ornithology, Ithaca New York
- Boo Weekley Charity Golf, Jay Florida
- Schultz Family Foundation, Emmaus Pennsylvania
- Mossy Oak Properties, West Point Mississippi
- Haas Outdoors, West Point Mississippi
- The Cupid Foundation, Baltimore Maryland
- Pennsylvania Outdoor Writer's Association, Harrisburg Pennsylvania
- Pennsylvania Taxidermy Association, Altoona Pennsylvania
- Cabela's, Hamburg Pennsylvania and Sidney Nebraska
- Parkland Jaycees, South Whitehall Pennsylvania

Partners

Product and Service Partners

- Joe Mascari Carpets and Rugs International, Allentown Pennsylvania
- Pennsylvania Taxidermy Association, Altoona Pennsylvania
- Cabela's, Hamburg Pennsylvania Sidney Nebraska
- Mossy Oak, West Point Mississippi
- Under Armour, Baltimore Maryland
- Leupold & Stevens, Beaverton Oregon
- Lehigh Valley Sporting Clays, Coplay Pennsylvania
- Professional Outdoor Media Association, Johnstown Pennsylvania

APPENDICES

- The Media Group, Bartlett Illinois
- Universal Hunter Magazine, Marietta Georgia
- North End, Guthsville, Grouse Hall, Ontelaunee Rod and Gun Clubs, Lehigh Valley Pennsylvania
- Levy Bus Company, Wescosville Pennsylvania
- Paul Smith's College, Paul Smith's New York
- Bass Pro Shops, Springfield Missouri
- Alps Outdoorz, New Haven Missouri
- Winchester, Morgan Utah
- Mill Creek Valley Game Calls, Corsica Pennsylvania
- Studio Bytes Web Site Building, Lehigh Valley Pennsylvania
- Tellox Web Hosting, Butler County Ohio
- Elk Mountain Inc., Shasta Lake California
- A.F. Boyer Hardware, Slatington Pennsylvania
- Higher Ground Tactical, Emmaus Pennsylvania
- Outdoor Cap Company, Bentonville Arkansas
- Trulock chokes, Whigham Georgia
- Iscope, Sikeston Missouri
- Heat Factory. Carlsbad California
- Thermacell, Bedford Massachusetts
- Synergy Outdoors, Baton Rouge Louisiana
- Henry Firearms, Bayonne New Jersey
- Rocky, Nelsonville Ohio
- Liberty Hollow Hunts, Lancaster Pennsylvania
- Buckwear, Baltimore Maryland
- Savage Firearms, Westfield Massachusetts
- Individual guest speakers, Varied Areas

B. Reward Types

Dinners

Reward dinners and meals provided by
- Cabela's in Hamburg, Pennsylvania
- Lehigh Valley Chapter of Safari Club International and Holiday Inn Conference Center, Fogelsville Pennsylvania
- Little Cesar's Pizza at Camp Compass, Allentown Pennsylvania
- Select restaurants, homes, and lodges via invitation

Field Rewards

- Big game hunts: Deer, Turkey, Boar and Bear
- Small game hunts: Squirrel, Pheasants, Dove, Rabbit and Crow
- Waterfowl hunts: Ducks and Geese
- Predator hunts: Fox and Coyote
- Freshwater fishing: Trout, Bass and Panfish
- Saltwater fishing: Flounder, Croaker, Weakfish, Stripers and Blue Fish
- Sporting clays: Using shotgun from various stations around a course to simulate wild game situations
- Trap and Skeet: Using shotgun from line of synchronized shooters that rotate to create various angles
- Novelty Shoots: Fun target practice done with both rifle and shotgun usually with themed targets
- Crossbow/Archery hunts: Deer
- Trap lines: Catching predators and furbearers via setting traps

- Lodge overnights: Sleeping in lodges to experience nights away usually combined with a hunt.
- Campfires: Time to reflect and share goals, food and dreams with Camp Compass members.
- Sporting events: Visiting traditional sporting events for a day. Professional baseball games are a good example.

Guides, Outfitters and Private Landowners Partners

- Full Fan Lodge, Montrose PA
- Pipeline Ridge, Muncy PA
- Mountaintop Whitetail Haven, Lykens PA
- B J Guide Service, Chestertown MD
- Rock Ridge, Pine Grove PA
- Bittner's Wild Wings, Kempton PA
- Settler's Safaris, Grahamstown South Africa
- Apex Outdoor Adventures, Kissimmee FL
- Kent Outdoors, Pottsboro TX
- Mountain Run Ranch, Hummelstown PA
- Clover Hollow, Slatington PA
- Randy Birch Waterfowling, Chincoteague VA
- Team Mayhem Waterfowling, Lehigh Valley, PA
- Indian Creek Farm, Danielsville PA
- Midwest Outfitters, Lynn KS
- Zip-Zim Sportfishing, Sodus Bay NY
- Ken Koury's River Adventures, Easton PA
- Biggie's Fishing Camp, Oswego NY
- Danny Santangelo, Lorida, FL
- Bent Creek Lodge, Jachin, AL
- Wrightway Outfitters Stony Plain, AB Canada

(cont.)
- Uncle Willie's Hunting Camp, Wilmington NC
- Savage Firearms, Westfield MA
- Private Landowners, Varied Areas

C. Program's Annual Calendar of Events

Date	Event	Description
09/10	Meeting	Roles/Responsibilities
09/17	Field Trip to LVSC	Shotgun Fine Arms Invitational
09/24	ICEP	Individualized Conservation Education Plan
10/01	PA Game Commission	Wildlife Notes 1 animal
10/15	PA Game Commission	Wildlife Notes 1 animal
10/22		Blood Trailing
10/29	Reward	Pizza Party
11/05	Conservation Orgs	
11/12		Black Bear
11/19	PA Hunting History	Deer Season
12/03	Shopping Sales tax	Cabela's Catalog
12/10		Dining Manners
12/17	Holiday Celebration	Cabela's
01/07		Lesson/ Ned Smith Sketch Book
01/14		Lesson/ Ned Smith Sketch Book
02/04		Lesson/ Ned Smith Sketch Book
02/11		Taxidermy
02/25		Taxidermy (Guest speaker)
03/04		Hunter Safety
03/18		Hunter Safety
03/25		Hunter Safety
04/08	Reward	Pizza Party
04/15		Turkey Topic
04/22		Thank you cards & letter writing
05/01		Addressing envelopes & postage
05/08	Rifle/North End	3:30 – 7:00
05/15	Rifle/North End	3:30 – 7:00
05/22	Shotgun LVSC	3:30 – 7:00
05/29	Shotgun LVSC	3:30 – 7:00
06/03	Annual Reflection/Last Day	Revisit ICEP 5:00 dismissal
06/03	Reward	Pizza Party
	Summer Trips as Offered	

The above table provides a general idea of our Academy's (after-school) schedule. It does not include the additional 12-20 reward events typically provided students during a program year.

D. Field Reports and How to Write Them

Creating the Report:

- ☑ Give the event a name.
- ☑ Identify where it takes place and who took part in the event.
- ☑ What did you expect to happen or what did you think you would get to do?
- ☑ Describe what actually did happen or what you did.
- ☑ How did you feel about the outcome?

Use "CUPS" to make the revision/editing checklist easier to remember:

C = Capitals
U = Understanding
P = Punctuation marks
S = Spelling

Sample Student Checklist for Field Reports

Use the checklist below to ask yourself the following questions about your report:

Revision Checklist:	Yes	No
1. Does my story make sense?		
2. Does it sound right when I read it out loud?		
3. Have I included enough detail so it is clear to someone who wasn't there?		
4. Does my story have a beginning, middle and an ending?		
5. Does my title match the story I've told?		
Editing Checklist:	Yes	No
1. Did I start each sentence with a capital?		
2. Did I remember to end each sentence with a period, an exclamation mark or a question mark?		
3. Did I use my dictionary to check my spelling?		
4. Did I show my work to someone else before turning it in or posting it?		

E. Personalized Help for You and/or Your Organization

John Annoni is available to help you or your organization by appointment. He will work with you one-on-one or arrange speaking engagements, seminars, or complete workshops based on his ideology, and proven work.

Pricing varies depending on the complexity of the engagement.

Contact the Author

How to reach John:
- Email: john@johnannoni.com
- Website (s):
    - campcompass.org
    - 2millionbullets.org
    - Johnannoni.com
- CCA Address:
    - 1221 Sumner Ave.
    - Allentown, PA 18102
- Paging system: 610-778-0576
- Donate online at campcompass.org
- Become a Bullet at 2millionbullets.org

My son Landon at age 6 (above), and today at age 16. He has grown into a good young man and I know the outdoors has played a positive role in his life. Special thanks to all of our extended outdoor family that helped him grow.

To learn more about my personal life, order my first book at johnannoni.com